BEAUTIFUL
Bullions
™

Contents

The Art of Bullion Stitches
A Bullion Stitch How-to Guide

BY **KATHRYN WHITE**

SKILL LEVEL
Intermediate–Advanced

MATERIALS
- Size 3 crochet cotton, or whatever thread or yarn you are comfortable with
- Size C/2/2.75mm in-line hook, or appropriate hook size for thread or yarn used

BULLION STITCHES
There is a special beauty to the bullion stitch (also known as the rolled stitch) that can't be duplicated by any other stitch. Most crocheters tend to be intimidated by this lovely stitch, which is a shame as it can add so much interest and dimension to a crocheted piece.

Its reputation of being difficult to do is poorly deserved. What normally makes it difficult is trying to do the stitch with the wrong type of hook or improper tension. Both are key factors in making the bullion stitch work.

Though a bullion stitch can be done with any hook, It is much easier to create if an in-line hook is used. There are some places that sell hooks just for this stitch. Unfortunately, I have only found them in limited sizes, but any in-line hook will get the job done.

What is an in-line hook, you ask? Good question. An in-line hook is a crochet hook that has the throat of the hook the same width or circumference as the shaft of the hook. It is easy to see if you hold the hook up so the hook is facing away from you. If it is an inline hook it will look the same from the hook head down to the thumb support.

If it tapers down from the hook head to the thumb support, it is not an in-line hook and will make doing a bullion stitch much more difficult as the loops tend to choke up around the throat of this type of hook, making it very difficult to draw the thread/yarn through.

I highly recommend using a hook that will give you the best chance of success.

The second most common error in trying to make a bullion stitch is tension. It is very easy to try to make your loops too tight or loose for the beginning loops and tighter for the ending loops. What works best is nice, relaxed, even loops that will allow you to draw your hook through easily.

First, let's look at the hook.

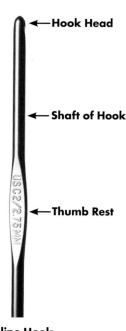

←Hook Head

←Shaft of Hook

USC2/2.75MM

←Thumb Rest

In-line Hook

WRAPS AROUND HOOK

When asked to do a bullion stitch in your piece, you will be told how many wraps to do. Sometimes it will give you an option of, say, 6–8 wraps. This is so you can decide what is easiest for you and gives you the best look. The number of wraps asked for can vary for different reasons.

The first reason is the height of the stitches around the bullion stitch—the more wraps, the higher your bullion stitch will be. So, if you have a double crochet next to your bullion stitch, you may be asked to do a 6-wrap bullion stitch. Whereas if you have a treble crochet next to it, you may be asked to do a 9-wrap bullion stitch.

The second reason may be the look. If you are using thread or a yarn that is smooth, then you may want to do a wrap or two more to make the bullion stitch look its best. As you get more proficient at making the bullion stitch, adding extra wraps to make the piece look its best will be no problem.

When you first start making bullion stitches, I recommend using the minimum number of wraps. This will make it easier for you to draw the hook through your loops. You can even reduce the number of wraps you do from what the pattern calls for until you get the hang of doing the stitch. This will make your bullion stitch a little less full but will allow you to accomplish the stitch more easily.

Whatever you decide, make sure you use it consistently throughout your piece. Once you have gained confidence with the stitch, you can do as many wraps as the pattern calls for with no problem.

But make it easiest for yourself to learn the stitch and gain confidence. A 5-wrap bullion stitch will teach you the basic idea and be easier to do than a 6-wrap.

When asked to do an 8-wrap bullion stitch, you will actually be drawing your thread through 10 loops when you do the stitch.

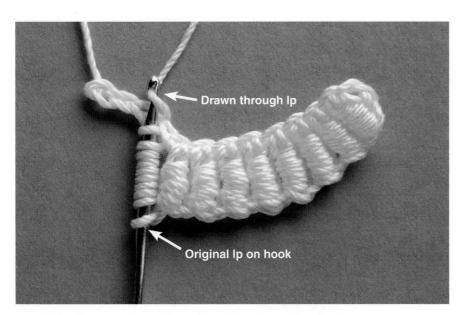

Drawn through lp

Original lp on hook

8-wrap bullion st ready to draw through 10 lps total on hook.

BULLION STITCH

Bullion stitch (bullion st): Wrap thread around hook the number of times indicated in the pattern, insert hook into st indicated, draw lp through, yo and draw through all lps on hook, do not draw up tight, yo and draw through lp to lock st.

Draw the hook with the lp on it through the looped wraps on the hook.

Wrap thread/yarn around hook number of times indicated—in this case, 8 wraps.

Insert hook into st indicated, draw lp through.

Check tension of lps at this point. Lps should be even and relaxed. Adjust lps at this point as necessary. Rotating the hook back and forth can help even out the tension. If you can't get the tension right, it is easier to try again rather than trying to pull the hook through too tight or uneven lps.

You may find it helpful to support the lps on the hook between the thumb and index finger as you draw the hook with the lp on it through the looped wraps on the hook. Draw through in a smooth, even manner. If your hook gets hung up, try rotating gently away from you. Don't rotate much at a time.

Thread has been drawn through. Do not pull up tight or you will crush your lps and the st will lose its nice clean look.

With practice, you should now be able to do the basic bullion st.

There are a few variations that you will need to know for the patterns in this book.

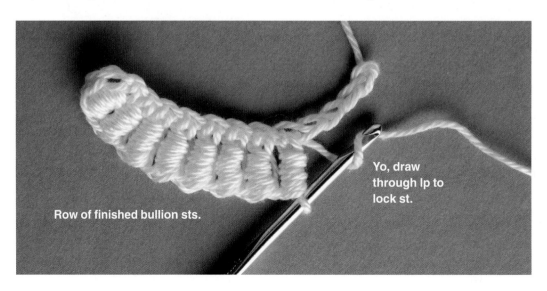

Row of finished bullion sts.

Yo, draw through lp to lock st.

FRONT POST BULLION STITCH

Front post bullion stitch (fp bullion st): Make a bullion st with number of wraps indicated with the thread caught up around the post of the st on the rnd before instead of into the top of the stitch. Complete as a bullion st.

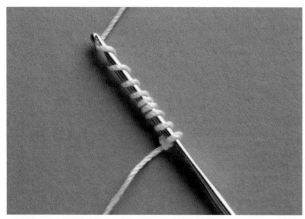

Wrap thread around hook as indicated.

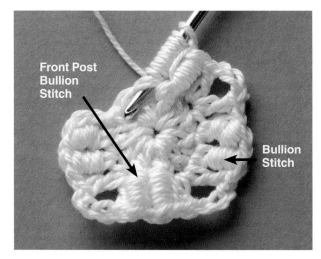

FREESTANDING BULLION STITCH

Freestanding bullion stitch (freestanding bullion st): Make a slip knot on your hook, wrap thread around hook the number of times indicated in the pattern, insert hook into st indicated, draw lp through, yo and draw through all lps on hook, do not draw up tight, yo and draw through lp to lock st.

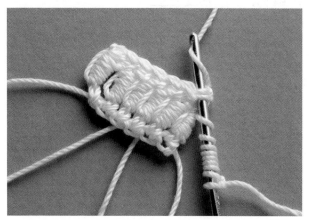

Insert hook into st indicated, draw lp through, finish bullion st in normal manner.

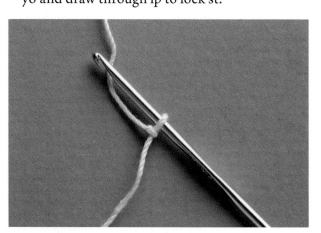

Place a slip knot on hook or whatever your method to begin in a ch st.

Finished Freestanding Bullion Stitch

Tradewinds Doily

SKILL LEVEL

INTERMEDIATE

FINISHED SIZE
14¾ inches in diameter

MATERIALS
- DMC Cebelia size 10 crochet cotton
  (1¾ oz/284 yds/50g per ball):
  175 yds #0210 violet
  75 yds #0001 white
- Nazli Gelin Garden 10 Metallic size 10
  cotton/metallic (306 yds/50g per ball):
  75 yds #12 purple/gold
- Size 7/1.65mm steel in-line crochet hook
  or size needed to obtain gauge
- Tapestry needle

GAUGE
Rnds 1–4 = 2⅛ inches in diameter; [bullion, dc]
5 times = 1⅛ inches

PATTERN NOTES
Weave in loose ends as work progresses.

When working bullion stitch, after drawing yarn
through indicated stitch, let the yarn relax for a
second before completing the stitch.

Maintain a fairly loose tension. Relax your
tension hand a little before drawing through
the loops.

When drawing the yarn through the loops,
try holding the hook open side down over the
first 2 stitches, and then rotate the hook so
the open side is facing up to draw through the
remain-ing loops.

Join with slip stitch as indicated unless otherwise stated.

Chain-2 at beginning of round counts as first
double crochet unless otherwise stated.

SPECIAL STITCHES
Bullion stitch (bullion st): Wrap yarn around hook
indicated number of times, insert hook in
indicated st, yo, draw up a lp, yo and gently
draw through all lps on hook, yo, do not draw
up tight, ch 1 to lock the st.

Front post bullion stitch (fp bullion st): Make bullion
st with indicated number of wraps with the
thread caught up around the post of indicated
st on rnd before by working front to back to
front around indicated st.

Triple picot (tr picot): Ch 4, sl st in front lp at top of
last st made, and the front strand of the actual
st of the same st, ch 5, sl st in the same st again,
catching the front lp of first ch-4 lp where sl st
in top of the st, ch 4, sl st in the same st again,
catching the front lp of the first ch-4 lp and
ch-5 lp where you sl st in top of the st.

Bullion shell: (7-wrap bullion sts in next ch-3 sp)
7 times.

Shell: (2 dc, ch 2, 2 dc) in indicted ch sp.

Beginning shell (beg shell): Sl st in next ch-2 sp,
(ch 2, dc, ch 2, 2 dc) in indicated ch sp.

Picot: Ch 3, sl st in indicated st.

DOILY

Rnd 1 (RS): With purple/gold, ch 5, **join** (see *Pattern Notes*) in first ch to form a ring, **ch 2** (see *Pattern Notes*), 17 dc in ring, join in beg ch-2. Fasten off. (*18 dc*)

Rnd 2: Join violet in any dc, ch 2, 7-wrap **fp bullion st** (see *Special Stitches*) in same st as beg ch-2, dc in same st, ch 3, sk next 2 dc, *(dc, 7-wrap fp bullion st, dc) in next dc, ch 3, sk next 2 dc, rep from * around, ending with join in beg ch-2. (*6 bullion sts, 12 dc, 6 ch-3 sps*)

Rnd 3: Ch 2, dc in same st, ch 3, sk bullion st, 2 dc in next dc, *ch 1**, 2 dc in next dc, ch 3, sk bullion st, 2 dc in next dc, rep from * around, ending last rep at ** with hdc in beg ch-2 to position hook for next rnd. (*24 dc, 6 ch-3 sps, 6 ch-1 sps*)

Rnd 4: Ch 1, sc in sp formed by hdc, *(7-wrap bullion st in next ch-3 sp) 6 times, sc in next ch-1 sp, rep from * around, join in first sc. Fasten off.

Rnd 5: Join white in sp between 3rd and 4th bullion st on any group of bullion sts, (ch 4, dc) in same sp, ch 3, (tr, 10-wrap bullion st, tr) in next sc, ch 3, *(dc, ch 2, dc) in sp between the 3rd and 4th bullion sts of next group of bullion sts, ch 3, (tr, 10-wrap bullion st, tr) in next sc, ch 3, rep from * around, join in 2nd ch of beg ch-4. (*6 bullion sts, 12 tr, 12 dc, 12 ch-3 sps*)

Rnd 6: Beg shell (see *Special Stitches*) in ch-2 sp, ch 4, sc in next tr, **fpsc** (see *Stitch Guide*) around next bullion st, ch 5, sl st in top of last sc made, sc in next tr, ch 4, ***shell** (see *Special Stitches*) in next ch-2 sp, ch 4, sc in next tr, fpsc around next bullion st, ch 5, sl st in top of last sc made, sc in next tr, ch 4, rep from * around, join in 2nd ch of beg ch-2. (*12 ch-4 sps, 6 ch-5 lps, 24 dc, 12 sc, 6 fpsc*)

Rnd 7: Beg shell in ch-2 sp, ch 4, shell in next ch-5 lp, ch 4, [shell in next ch 2-sp, ch 4, shell in next ch-5 lp, ch 4] around, join in 2nd ch of beg ch-2. (*12 shells, 12 ch-4 sps*)

Rnd 8: Beg shell in ch-2 sp, ch 5, [shell in next ch-2 sp, ch 5] around, join in beg ch-2. (*12 shells, 12 ch-5 sps*)

Rnd 9: Ch 2, dc in next dc, 3 dc in next ch-2 sp, dc in each of next 2 dc, 5 dc in next ch-5 sp, [dc in each of next 2 dc, 3 dc in next ch-2 sp, dc in each of next 2 dc, 5 dc in next ch-5 sp] around, join in 2nd ch of beg ch-2. Fasten off. (*144 dc*)

Rnd 10: Join purple/gold in **front lp** (*see Stitch Guide*) of first dc of rnd, ch 1, sc in same st, working in front lp around, sc in next dc, **dtr** (*see Stitch Guide*) in next ch-2 sp of rnd 7, sc in next 3 dc, dtr in same ch-2 sp of rnd 7, [sc in each of next 9 dc, dtr in next ch-2 sp of rnd 7, sc in next 3 dc, dtr in same ch-2 sp of rnd 7] around, ending with sc in next 7 sc, join in first sc of rnd. Fasten off.

Rnd 11: Join violet in **back lp** (*see Stitch Guide*) of the 2nd dc worked in any ch-2 sp on rnd 9, ch 1, sc in same st, working in back lp, sc in each dc around, join in beg sc. (*144 sc*)

Rnd 12: Ch 5, sk next 2 sc, sc in next sc, ch 6, sk next 5 sc, sc in next sc, ch 3, sk next 2 sc, [dc in next sc, ch 3, sk next 2 sc, sc in next sc, ch 6, sk next 5 sc, sc in next sc, ch 3, sk next 2 sc] around, join in 2nd ch of beg ch-5. (*12 dc, 12 ch-6 sps, 24 ch-3 sps*)

Rnd 13: (Ch 2, 7-wrap bullion st, dc) in same st, ch 4, (sc, ch 2, sc) in next ch-6 sp, ch 4, [(dc, 7-wrap bullion st, dc) in next dc, ch 4, (sc, ch 2, sc) in next ch-6 sp, around, join in 2nd ch of beg ch-2. (*12 bullion sts*)

Rnd 14: Ch 2, dc in same st, ch 3, sk bullion st, 2 dc in next dc, ch 4, dc in next ch-2 sp, [ch 4, 2 dc in next dc, ch 3, sk bullion st, 2 dc in next dc, ch 4, dc in next ch-2 sp] around, ending with ch 2, dc in 2nd ch of beg ch-2 to position hook in center of last lp.

Rnd 15: Ch 1, sc in same sp, ***bullion shell** (*see Special Stitches*) in next ch-3 sp, sc in next ch-4 sp, ch 2, 3 dc in next dc, ch 2**, sc in next ch-4 sp, rep from * around, ending last rep at **, join in beg sc. Fasten off. (*12 pineapple bases*)

Rnd 16: Join violet around first dc of any 3-dc group, ch 2, *(dc, ch 2, dc) in next dc, **fpdc** (*see Stitch Guide*) around next dc, ch 2, sc between first and 2nd bullion sts, [ch 3, sc in sp between next bullion sts] 5 times, ch 2**, fpdc in next dc, rep from * around, ending last rep at **, join in 2nd ch of beg ch-2.

Rnd 17: Sl st around next dc, ch 2, *(dc, ch 2, dc) in next ch-2 sp, fpdc around next dc, ch 2, sc in next ch-3 sp, [ch 3, sc in next ch-3 sp] 4 times, ch 2, sk next fpdc**, fpdc around next dc, rep from * around, ending last rep at **, join in beg ch-2.

Rnd 18: Sl st around next dc, ch 2, *(dc, ch 1, 2 dc, ch 1, dc) in next ch-2 sp, fpdc around next dc, ch 2, sc in next ch-3 sp, [ch 3, sc in next ch-3 sp] 3 times, ch 2, sk next fpdc**, fpdc around next dc, rep from * around, ending last rep at **, join in beg ch-2.

Rnd 19: Sl st around next dc, ch 2, *(dc, ch 2, dc) in next ch-1 sp, fpdc around each of next 2 dc, (dc, ch 2, dc) in next ch-1 sp, fpdc around next dc, ch 2, sc in next ch-3 sp, [ch 3, sc in next ch-3 sp] twice, ch 2, sk next fpdc**, fpdc around next dc, rep from * around, ending last rep at **, join in beg ch-2.

Rnd 20: Sl st around next dc, ch 2, *(dc, ch 2, dc) in next ch-2 sp, fpdc around next dc, ch 4, sk next 2 fpdc, fpdc around next dc, (dc, ch 2, dc) in next ch-2 sp, fpdc around next dc, ch 2, sc in next ch-3 sp, ch 3, sc in next ch-3 sp, ch 2, sk next fpdc**, fpdc around next dc, rep from * around, ending last rep at **, join in beg ch-2.

Rnd 21: Sl st around next dc, ch 2, *(dc, ch 2, dc) in next ch-2 sp, fpdc around next dc, ch 4, dc in next ch-4 sp, ch 4, sk next fpdc, fpdc around next dc, (dc, ch 2, dc) in next ch-2 sp, fpdc around next dc, ch 2, sc in next ch-3 sp, ch 2, sk next fpdc**, fpdc around next dc, rep from * around, ending last rep at **, join in beg ch-2.

Rnd 22: Sl st around next dc, ch 2, *(dc, ch 2, dc) in next ch-2 sp, fpdc around next dc, ch 5, sk next fpdc, (dc, 7-wrap bullion st, dc) in next dc, ch 5, sk next fpdc, fpdc around next dc, (dc, ch 2, dc) in next ch-2 sp, fpdc around next dc, ch 1, sk next 2 fpdc**, fpdc around next dc, rep from * around, ending last rep at **, join in beg ch-2.

Rnd 23: Sl st around next dc, ch 2, holding the last lp of each st on the hook, **fptr** *(see Stitch Guide)* in next dc, tr in next ch-2 sp, yo, draw through all 3 lps on hook, *ch 7, sk next dc, sk next fpdc, 2 dc in next dc, ch 3, sk next bullion st, 2 dc in next dc, ch 7, sk next fpdc, sk next dc, holding last lp of each st on the hook, tr in next ch-2 sp, fptr in next dc, tr in next fpdc, tr in ch-1 sp, tr in next fpdc, fptr in next dc, tr in next ch-2 sp, yo, draw though all 8 lps on hook, rep from * around, ending with ch 7, sk next dc, sk next fpdc, 2 dc in next dc, ch 3, sk next bullion st, 2 dc in next dc, ch 7, sk next fpdc, sk next dc, holding the last lp of each st on the hook, tr in next ch-2 sp, fptr in next dc, tr in next fpdc, tr in ch-1 sp, yo, draw though all 5 lps on hook, join in beg ch-2. Fasten off. *(12 cls)*

Rnd 24: Join purple/gold in tip of any cluster, ch 1, sc in same st, *8 sc in next ch-7 sp, sc in each of next 2 dc, 3 sc in next ch-3 sp, sc in each of next 2 dc, 8 dc in next ch-7 sp**, sc in tip of next cluster, rep from * around, ending with last rep at **, join in beg sc.

Rnd 25: Ch 1, sc in same st, working in front lp, ch 2, sk next st, [sc in next st, ch 2, sk next st] around, join in beg sc. Fasten off.

Rnd 26: Join white in back lp of first sc of rnd 24, working in back lp, ch 2, 7-wrap bullion st in next sc, [dc in next sc, 7-wrap bullion st in next st] around, join in beg ch-2.

Rnd 27: Ch 1, sc in same st, sc in next bullion st, [sc in next dc, sc in next bullion st] around, join in beg sc. Fasten off.

Rnd 28: Join purple/gold in front lp of first sc of rnd 27, ch 1, sc in same st, working in front lp, ch 2, sk next sc, [sc in next sc, ch 2, sk next sc] around, join in beg sc.

Rnd 29: Sl st in back lp of rnd 28, ch 1, sc in same st, working in back lp, sc in each st around, join in beg sc. Fasten off.

Rnd 30: Join violet in sc that is in line with the 2nd sc in any ch-3 sp on rnd 23, ch 1, sc in same sc, sc in each rem sc around, join in beg sc.

Rnd 31: (Ch 2, 7-wrap bullion st, dc) in same sc, ch 3, sk next 3 sc, sc in next sc, ch 3, sk next 3 sc, [(dc, 7-wrap bullion st, dc) in next sc, ch 3, sk next 3 sc, sc in next sc, ch 3, sk next 3 sc] around, join in beg ch-2.

Rnd 32: Ch 2, dc in same st, ch 3, 2 dc in next dc, [ch 3, 2 dc in next dc, ch 3, 2 dc in next dc] around, ending with ch 1, dc in 2nd ch of beg ch-2.

Rnd 33: Ch 1, sc in same sp, (7-wrap bullion sts) 6 times in next ch-3 sp, [sc in next ch-3 sp, (7-wrap bullion sts) 6 times in next ch-3 sp] around, join in beg sc. Fasten off.

Rnd 34: Join purple/gold in any sc between groups of bullion sts, ch 1, sc in same st, *sc in sp before first bullion st, 2 sc in next sp between bullion sts, sc in next sp between bullion sts, **picot** *(see Special Stitches)* in last sc made, sc in same sp, 2 sc in next sp between bullion sts, **triple picot** *(see Special Stitches)* in last sc made, sc in same sp, sc in next sp between bullion sts, picot in last sc made, sc in same sp, 2 sc in next sp between bullion sts, sc in sp after last bullion st**, sc in next sc, rep from * around, ending last rep at **, join in beg sc. Fasten off.

Block Doily. ∎

Pieces of Eight
Doily

EXPERIENCED

FINISHED SIZE
10 inches square

MATERIALS
- DMC Cebelia size 10 crochet cotton (1¾ oz/284 yds/50g per ball): 2 balls #0002 ecru
- Size 7/1.65mm in-line steel crochet hook or size needed to obtain gauge
- Tapestry needle
- 4 stitch markers

GAUGE
Rnds 1–11 = 3¾ inches square; 11 dc = 1 inch; 1 dc rnd = ⅜ inch

PATTERN NOTES
Weave in loose ends as work progresses.

Join with slip stitch as indicated unless otherwise stated.

When working bullion stitch, after drawing yarn through indicated stitch, let the yarn relax for a second before completing the stitch.

Maintain a fairly loose tension. Relax your tension hand a little before drawing through the loops.

When drawing the yarn through the loops, try holding the hook open side down the first 2 stitches, and then rotate the hook so the open side is facing up to draw through the remaining loops.

Chain-3 at beginning of round counts as first treble crochet unless otherwise stated.

Chain-8 at beginning of round counts as first triple treble crochet and chain 2 unless otherwise stated.

SPECIAL STITCHES
Bullion stitch (bullion st): Wrap yarn around hook 7 times, insert hook in indicated st, yo, draw up lp, yo and gently draw through all lps on hook, yo, do not draw up tight, ch 1 to lock st.

Triple treble crochet (trtr): Yo hook 4 times, insert hook in indicated st, yo, draw up lp, [yo, draw through 2 lps on hook] 5 times.

Extended double crochet (edc): Yo, insert hook in indicated st, yo, draw up lp, yo, draw through 1 lp, [yo, draw through 2 lps on hook] twice.

Triple picot (tr picot): Ch 4, sl st in front lp at top of last st made and front strand of the same st, ch 5, sl st in the same st again, catching the front lp of first ch-4 lp where sl st in top of the st was worked, ch 4, sl st in the same st again, catching the front lp of the first ch-4 lp and ch-5 lp where sl st in top of st was worked.

Chain-4 picot (ch-4 picot): Ch 4, sl st in first ch of ch-4.

Chain-3 picot (ch-3 picot): Ch 3, sl st in top of last st made.

3-treble crochet cluster (3-tr cl): *[Yo hook twice, insert hook in indicated st or sp, yo, draw up lp, yo, draw through 2 lps on hook] twice, rep from * twice, yo, draw through rem 4 lps on hook.

Beginning 3-treble crochet cluster (beg 3-tr cl): Ch 2, *[yo hook twice, insert hook in indicated st or sp, yo, draw up lp, yo, draw through 2 lps on hook] twice, rep from * once, yo, draw through rem 3 lps on hook.

DOILY

Rnd 1 (RS): Ch 5, **join** (see Pattern Notes) in first ch to form ring, ch 1, 8 sc in ring, join in **back lp** (see Stitch Guide) of first sc. (8 sc)

Rnd 2: Working in back lp, ch 1, sc in same sc as beg ch-1, **bullion st** (see Special Stitches) in same sc as beg ch-1, (sc, bullion st) in each of next 7 sc, join in beg sc. (8 bullion sts, 8 sc)

Rnd 3: Ch 1, sc in same sc, [ch 4, sc in next sc] 7 times, ch 1, **edc** (see Special Stitches) in first sc to form last ch-4 sp. (8 ch-4 sps, 8 sc)

Rnd 4: Ch 1, (sc, ch 6, sc) in same sp, *[ch 4, sc in next ch-4 sp] twice, ch 6, sc in same ch-4 sp, rep from * twice, ch 4, sc in next ch-4 sp, ch 1, edc in beg sc. (4 ch-6 sps, 8 ch-4 sps)

Rnd 5: Ch 1, sc in same sp, ch 4, (sc, ch 6, sc) in next ch-6 sp, *[ch 4, sc in next ch-4 sp] twice, ch 4, (sc, ch 6, sc) in next ch-6 sp, rep from * twice, ch 4, sc in next ch-4 sp, ch 1, edc in beg sc. (4 ch-6 sps, 12 ch-4 sps)

Rnd 6: Ch 1, sc in same sp, ch 4, sc in next ch-4 sp, ch 4, (sc, ch 6, sc) in next ch-6 sp, *[ch 4, sc in next ch-4 sp] 3 times, ch 4, (sc, ch 6, sc) in next ch-6 sp, rep from * twice, ch 4, sc in next ch-4 sp, ch 1, edc in beg sc. (4 ch-6 sps, 16 ch-4 sps)

Rnd 7: Ch 1, sc in same sp, [ch 4, sc in next ch-4 sp] twice, ch 4, (sc, ch 6, sc) in next ch-6 sp, *[ch 4, sc in next ch-4 sp] 4 times, ch 4, (sc, ch 6, sc) in next ch-6 sp, rep from * twice, ch 4, sc in next ch-4 sp, ch 4, join beg sc. (4 ch-6 sps, 20 ch-4 sps)

Rnd 8: Sl st in next ch-4 sp, ch 1, 3 sc in same sp, 4 sc in next ch-4 sp, 3 sc in next ch-4 sp, *7 sc in next ch-6 sp, [3 sc in next ch-4 sp, 4 sc in next ch-4 sp] twice, 3 sc in next ch-4 sp, rep from * around, ending with 3 sc in next ch-4 sp, 4 sc in next ch-4 sp, sl st into back lp of beg sc. (96 sc)

Rnd 9: Ch 1, working in back lp, sc in each of next 13 sc, 3 sc in next sc, [sc in each of next 23 sc, 3 sc in next sc] around, ending with sc in each of next 10 sc, join in beg sc. (104 sc)

Rnd 10: With in-line hook, ch 1, sc in same st, bullion st in front lp of 2nd st of rnd 8, sk next sc on rnd 9, sc in next sc, [sk next st on rnd 8, bullion st in front lp of next st on rnd 8, sk next sc on rnd 9, sc in next sc] 6 times,

   A. bullion st in same st on rnd 8, sk next sc on rnd 9, sc in next sc, bullion st in same st on rnd 8, sk next sc on rnd 9, sc in next sc;

   B. *[sk next st on rnd 8, bullion st in front lp of next st on rnd 8, sk next sc on rnd 9, sc in next sc] 12 times, bullion st in same st on rnd 8, sk next sc on rnd 9, sc in next sc, bullion st in same st on rnd 8, sk next sc on rnd 9, sc in next sc, rep from * around;

   C. ending with [sk next st on rnd 8, bullion st in front lp of next st on rnd 8, sk next sc on rnd 9, sc in next sc] 5 times, sk next st on rnd 8, bullion st in front lp of next st on rnd 8, join in beg sc. (56 bullion sts)

Rnd 11: Ch 1, sc in same sc, [sc in top of next bullion st, sc in next sc] 7 times, 3 sc in top of next bullion st, sc in next sc, *[sc in top of next bullion st, sc in next sc] 13 times, 3 sc in top of next bullion st, sc in next sc, rep from * around, ending with [sc in top of next bullion st, sc in next sc] 5 times, sc in top of next bullion st, join in beg sc. (120 sc)

Rnd 12: Sl st into next sc, (**ch 2**—see Pattern Notes, dc, ch 3, 2 dc) in same st (for side shell), ch 2, sk next 3 sc, sc in next sc, ch 2, sk next 3 sc, (dc, ch 3, dc) in next sc, ch 2, sk next 3 sc, sc in next sc, ch 3, sk next 2 sc,

A. (2 tr, ch 3, 2 tr) in next sc *(for corner shell)*, ch 3, sk next 2 sc, sc in next sc, ch 2, sk next 3 sc, (dc, ch 3, dc) in next sc, ch 2, sk next 3 sc, sc in next sc, ch 2;

B. *sk next 3 sc, (2 dc, ch 3, 2 dc) in next sc *(for side shell)*, ch 2, sk next 3 sc, sc in next sc, ch 2, sk next 3 sc, (dc, ch 3, dc) in next sc, ch 2, sk next 3 sc, sc in next sc, ch 3, sk next 2 sc, (2 tr, ch 3, 2 tr) in next sc *(for corner shell)*, ch 3, sk next 2 sc, sc in next sc, ch 2, sk next 3 sc, (dc, ch 3, dc) in next sc, ch 2, sk next 3 sc, sc in next sc, ch 2, rep from * around, join in beg ch-2. *(4 corner shells, 4 side shells)*

Rnd 13: Sl st into next ch-3 sp, **ch 3** *(see Pattern Notes)*, tr in same sp, (ch 2, 2 dc in same ch-3 sp) twice, ch 2, 2 tr in same ch-3 sp, ch 3, (dc, ch 3, dc) in next ch-3 sp,

A. ch 3, sk next ch-3 sp, 2 tr in next ch-3 sp, (ch 3, 2 tr in same ch-3 sp) 3 times, ch 3, sk next ch-3 sp, (dc, ch 3, dc) in next ch-3 sp, ch 3;

B. *2 tr in next ch-3 sp, (ch 2, 2 dc in same ch-3 sp) twice, ch 2, 2 tr in same ch-3 sp, ch 3, (dc, ch 3, dc) in next ch-3 sp, ch 3, sk next ch-3 sp, 2 tr in next ch-3 sp, (ch 3, 2 tr in same sp) 3 times, ch 3, sk next ch-3 sp, (dc, ch 3, dc) in next ch-3 sp, ch 3, rep from * around, join in 3rd ch of beg, ch 3.

Rnd 14: Sl st into ch-2 sp, ch 3, tr in same sp, (ch 2, 2 dc) in same ch-2 sp, ch 1, (2 dc, ch 2, 2 dc) in next ch-2 sp, ch 1, (2 dc, ch 2, 2 tr) in next ch-2 sp, ch 1, sk next ch-3 sp, dc in next ch-3 sp, **ch-4 picot** *(see Special Stitches)*, ch 1, dc in same ch-3 sp,

A. ch 1, sk next ch-3 sp, (2 tr, ch 2, 2 tr) in next ch-3 sp, ch 1, 2 tr in next ch-3 sp, (ch 2, 2 tr in same ch-3 sp) 3 times, ch 1, (2 tr, ch 2, 2 tr) in next ch-2 sp, ch 1, sk next ch-3 sp, (dc, ch-4 picot, ch 1, dc) in next ch-3 sp, ch 1, sk next ch-3 sp;

B. *(2 tr, ch 2, 2 dc) in next ch-3 sp, ch 1, (2 dc, ch 2, 2 dc) in next ch-2 sp, ch 1, (2 dc, ch 2, 2 tr) in next ch-2 sp, ch 1, sk next ch-3 sp, (dc, ch-4 picot, ch 1, dc) in next ch 3 sp, ch 1, sk next ch-3 sp, (2 tr, ch 2, 2 tr) in next ch-3

sp, ch 1, 2 tr in next ch-3 sp, (ch 2, 2 tr in same sp) 3 times, ch 1, (2 tr, ch 2, 2 tr) in next ch-2 sp, ch 1, sk next ch-3 sp, (dc, ch-4 picot, ch 1, dc) in next ch-3 sp, ch 1, sk next ch-3 sp, rep from * around, join in beg ch-3.

Rnd 15: Sl st into next ch-2 sp, **beg 3-tr cl** *(see Special Stitches)* in same ch-2 sp, **ch-3 picot** *(see Special Stitches)* in top of cl, ch 2, **3-tr cl** *(see Special Stitches)* in same ch-2 sp, ch-3 picot in top of cl, ch 2, 3-tr cl, ch-3 picot in top of cl in next ch-2 sp, (ch 2, 3-tr cl, ch-3 picot in same ch-2 sp) twice,

A. [(ch 2, 3-tr cl, ch-3 picot in top of last cl, ch 2, 3-tr cl, ch-3 picot in top of last cl) in next ch-2 sp] 6 times;

B. *(ch 2, 3-tr cluster, ch-3 picot in top of last cl, ch 2, 3-tr cl, ch-3 picot in top of last cl) in next ch-2 sp, ch 2, 3-tr cl, ch-3 picot in top of last cl in next ch-2 sp, (ch 2, 3-tr cl, ch-3 picot in same sp) twice;

C. [(ch 2, 3-tr cl, ch-3 picot in top of last cl, ch 2, 3-tr cl, ch-3 picot in top of last cl) in next ch-2 sp] 6 times, rep from * around, ending with ch 1, hdc into top of first cl to position hook in center of last ch sp.

Rnd 16: Ch 8 *(see Pattern Notes)*, dtr in next ch-2 sp, ch 2, tr in next ch-2 sp, [ch 2, dc in next ch-2 sp] twice, ch 2, tr in next ch-2 sp, ch 2, dtr in next ch-2 sp, ch 2, **trtr** *(see Special Stitches)* in next ch-2 sp, ch 2, dtr in next ch-2 sp,

A. [ch 2, tr in next ch-2 sp] 4 times, (ch 2, dtr, ch 3, dtr, ch 2, tr) in same ch-2 sp, [ch 2, tr in next ch-2 sp] 3 times, ch 2, dtr in next ch-2 sp, ch 2;

B. *trtr in next ch-2 sp, ch 2, dtr in next ch-2 sp, ch 2, tr in next ch-2 sp, [ch 2, dc in next ch-2 sp] twice, ch 2, tr in next ch-2 sp, ch 2, dtr in next ch-2 sp, ch 2, trtr in next ch-2 sp, ch 2, dtr in next ch-2 sp, [ch 2, tr in next ch-2 sp] 4 times, (ch 2, dtr, ch 3, dtr, ch 2, tr) in same ch-2 sp, [ch 2, tr in next ch-2 sp] 3 times, ch 2, dtr in next ch-2 sp, ch 2, rep from * around, join in 6th ch of beg ch-8. *(80 sts, 76 ch-2 sps, 4 ch-3 sps)*

Rnd 17: Sl st into ch-2 sp, ch 1, 3 sc in same sp, [3 sc in next ch-2 sp] 12 times, 5 sc in next ch-3 sp, *[3 sc in next ch-2 sp] 19 times, 5 sc in next ch-3 sp, rep from * around, ending with [3 sc in next ch-2 sp] 6 times, sl st in back lp of beg sc. (248 sc)

Rnd 18: Working in back lp, ch 1, sc in same st, sc in each of next 40 sc, 3 sc in next sc, *sc in each of next 61 sc, 3 sc in next sc, rep from * around, ending with sc in each of next 20 sc, join in beg sc. (256 sc)

Rnd 19: With in-line hook, ch 1, sc in same st, bullion st in the front lp of 2nd st of rnd 17, sk next sc on rnd 18, sc in next sc, [sk next st on rnd 17, bullion st in front lp of next st on rnd 17, sk next sc on rnd 18, sc in next sc] 20 times, (bullion st in same st, sc in next sc on rnd 18) twice,

A. *[sk next st on rnd 17, bullion st in front lp of next st on rnd 17, sk next sc on rnd 18, sc in next sc] 31 times, (bullion st in same st, sc in next sc on rnd 18) twice, rep from * around;

B. ending with [sk next st on rnd 17, bullion st in front lp of next st on rnd 17, sk next sc on rnd 18, sc in next sc] 8 times, sk next st on rnd 17, bullion st in front lp of next st on rnd 17, sk next sc on rnd 18, join in beg sc.

Rnd 20: Ch 1, sc in same sc, sc in top of next bullion st, [sc in next sc, sc in top of next bullion st] 20 times, sc in next sc, 4 sc in top of next bullion st *(this will be the center bullion st in corner; mark the 3rd sc with stitch marker)*, *[sc in next sc, sc in top of next bullion st] 32 times, sc in next sc, 4 sc in top of next bullion st, *(this will be the center bullion st in corner; mark the 3rd sc with stitch marker)*, rep from * around, ending with [sc in next sc, sc in top of next bullion st] 11 times, join in beg sc. Fasten off.

FIRST CORNER

Row 1: Count back 20 sts from marked sc in any corner, join thread in this st, ch 1, sc in same sc, now working toward the same marked corner st, [ch 4, sk next 3 sc, sc in next sc] 5 times *(last sc will be in the marked sc)*, ch 6, sc in same sc, [ch 4, sk next 3 sc, sc in next sc] 5 times, turn. *(10 ch-4 sps, 1 ch-6 corner sp)*

Row 2: Ch 4, sc in first ch-4 sp, [ch 4, sc in next ch-4 sp] 4 times, ch 4, (sc, ch 6, sc) in ch-6 sp, [ch 4, sc in next ch-4 sp] 5 times, ch 2, dc in first sc to form last ch-5 sp, turn.

Row 3: Ch 1, sc in dc, [ch 4, sc in next ch-4 sp] 5 times, ch 4, (sc, ch 6, sc) in next ch-6 sp, [ch 4, sc in next ch-4 sp] 6 times, turn.

Row 4: Ch 4, sc in first ch-4 sp, [ch 4, sc in next ch-4 sp] 5 times, ch 4, (sc, ch 6, sc) in ch-6 sp, [ch 4, sc in next ch-4 sp] 6 times, ch 2, dc in first sc to form last ch-5 sp, turn.

Row 5: Ch 1, sc in dc, [ch 4, sc in next ch-4 sp] 6 times, ch 4, (sc, ch 6, sc) in next ch-6 sp, [ch 4, sc in next ch-4 sp] 7 times, turn.

Row 6: Ch 4, sc in first ch-4 sp, [ch 4, sc in next ch-4 sp] 6 times, ch 4, (sc, ch 6, sc) in ch-6 sp, [ch 4, sc in next ch-4 sp] 7 times, ch 2, dc in first sc to form last ch-5 sp. Fasten off. *(16 ch-4 sps, 1 ch-6 sp)*

Row 7: With right side facing, join thread in first sc on rnd 20 just before the mesh corner, ch 1, sc in same sc, 3 sc in end mesh on row 2, 3 sc in mesh on end of row 4, 7 sc in first mesh of row 6, [3 sc in next ch-4 sp] 7 times, 7 sc in next ch-6 sp, [3 sc in next ch-4 sp] 7 times, 7 sc in last mesh of row 6, 3 sc in the mesh on end of row 4, 3 sc in the end mesh on row 2, sc in next sc on rnd 20, sl st in next sc on rnd 20, turn. *(77 sc)*

Row 8: Ch 1, working in **front lp** *(see Stitch Guide)* across, sk next sc, sc in next 8 sc, 2 sc in next sc, sc in next sc, 2 sc in next sc, [sc in each of next 25 sc, 2 sc in next sc, sc in next sc, 2 sc in next sc] twice, sc in next 8 sc, sk next sc, sl st in next sc, turn. *(81 sc)*

Row 9: With in-line hook, sl st in next sc, ch 1, sc in next sc, sk first sc in mesh on row 7, bullion st in front lp of next sc, sk next sc on row 8, sc in next sc,

A. [sk next sc on row 7, bullion st in front lp of next sc, sk next sc on row 8, sc in next sc] 3 times, sk next sc on row 7, bullion st in front lp of next sc, sc in next sc on row 8, bullion st in same st, sc in next sc on row 8, bullion st in same st, sk next sc on row 8, sc in next sc;

B. {[sk next sc on row 7, bullion st in front lp of next sc, sk next sc on row 8, sc in next sc] 12 times, sk next sc on row 7, bullion st in front lp of next sc, sc in next sc on row 8, bullion st in same st, sc in next sc on row 8, bullion st in same st, sk next sc on row 8, sc in next sc} twice;

C. [sk next sc on row 7, bullion st in front lp of next sc, sk next sc on row 8, sc in next sc] 4 times, sc in next sc on rnd 20. Fasten off. *(43 bullion sts)*

Row 10: With right side facing, join thread in first sc on rnd 20 *(just before the mesh corner)*, ch 1, sc in same sc, [sc in next sc, sc in top of next bullion st] 5 times, sc in next sc, 4 sc in next bullion st, {[sc in next sc, sc in top of next bullion st] 15 times, sc in next sc, 4 sc in next bullion st} twice, [sc in next sc, sc in top of next bullion st] 5 times, sl st in next sc on rnd 20. Fasten off.

REM 3 CORNERS
Rep rows 1–10 on each of rem 3 corners. After 4th corner is completed, **do not fasten off.**

BORDER
Rnd 21: Ch 1, sc in each of next 5 sc, ch 4, sk each of next 4 sc on rnd 20, (3-tr cl, ch 4, 3-tr cl) in next sc *(this will be the center sc on this side)*, ch 4, sk next 4 sc, sc in each of next 5 sc, sc in first sc on corner, [ch 4, sk next 3 sc, sc in next sc] 3 times, ch 6, sc in same sc,

A. [ch 4, sk next 3 sc, sc in next sc] 8 times, ch 4, sk next 2 sc, sc in next sc, ch 6 sc in same sc, ch 4, sk next 2 sc, sc in next sc, [ch 4, sk next 3 sc, sc in next sc] 8 times, ch 6, sc in same sc, [ch 4, sk next 3 sc, sc in next sc] 3 times;

B. *sc in next 5 sc on rnd 20, ch 4, sk next 4 sc on rnd 20, (3-tr cl, ch 4, 3-tr cl) in next sc *(this will be center sc on this side)*, ch 4, sk next 4 sc, sc in each of next 5 sc, sc in first sc on corner, [ch 4, sk next 3 sc, sc in next sc] 3 times, ch 6, sc in same sc, [ch 4, sk next 3 sc, sc in next sc] 8 times;

C. ch 4, sk next 2 sc, sc in next sc, ch 6, sc in same sc, ch 4, sk next 2 sc, sc in next sc, [ch 4, sk next 3 sc, sc in next sc] 8 times, ch 6, sc in same sc, [ch 4, sk next 3 sc, sc in next sc] 3 times, rep from * around, join in beg sc.

Rnd 22: Sl st into next sc, ch 1, sc in each of next 3 sc, (3 sc, ch-3 picot in last sc made, 2 sc) in next ch-4 sp, sc in top of cl, (3 sc, **tr picot**—*see Special Stitches* in last sc made, 2 sc) in next ch-4 sp, sc in top of next cl, (3 sc, ch-3 picot in last sc made, 2 sc) in next ch-4 sp,

A. sk sc at base of ch-4, sc in next 3 sc, [(3 sc, ch-3 picot in last sc made, 2 sc) in next ch-4 sp] 3 times, (4 sc, triple picot in last sc made, 3 sc) in next ch-6 sp;

B. [(3 sc, ch-3 picot in last sc made, 2 sc) in next ch-4 sp) 9 times, (4 sc, triple picot in last sc made, 3 sc) in next ch-6 sp] twice, [(3 sc, ch-3 picot in last sc made, 2 sc) in next ch-4 sp] 3 times, sk next sc at base of ch-4;

C. *sc in next 3 sc, (3 sc, ch-3 picot in last sc made, 2 sc) in next ch-4 sp, sc in top of cl, (3 sc, triple picot in last sc made, 2 sc) in next ch-4 sp, sc in top of next cl, (3 sc, ch-3 picot in last sc made, 2 sc) in next ch-4 sp, sk sc at base of ch-4;

D. sc in next 3 sc, [(3 sc, ch-3 picot in last sc made, 2 sc) in next ch-4 sp] 3 times, (4 sc, triple picot in last sc made, 3 sc) in next ch-6 sp, [(3 sc, ch-3 picot in last sc made, 2 sc) in next ch-4 sp] 9 times;

E. [(4 sc, triple picot in last sc made, 3 sc) in next ch-6 sp] twice, [(3 sc, ch-3 picot in last sc made, 2 sc) in next ch-4 sp] 3 times, sk next sc at base of ch-4, rep from * around, ending with join in beg sc. Fasten off. Block Doily. ■

Bullion Star
Necklace

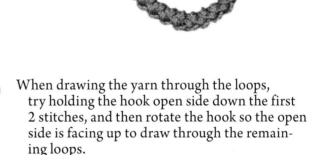

SKILL LEVEL

INTERMEDIATE

FINISHED SIZES

Choker: small *(16 inches)*; changes for medium *(18 inches)* and large *(20 inches)* are in [ ].

MATERIALS

- Lizbeth thread size 10: (122 yds per ball):
    - 40 yds #640 antique violet medium
    - 25 yds #664 ocean teal medium
    - 10 yds #676 leaf green dark
- Sizes 7/1.65mm and 5/1.90mm in-line steel crochet hooks or sizes needed to obtain gauge
- Sewing needle
- 2mm pearl beads: 4
- 4mm pearl bead

GAUGE

Flower measures 1¾ inches across

PATTERN NOTES

Weave in loose ends as work progresses.

Join with slip stitch as indicated unless otherwise stated.

Use care to use sewing needle that will pass through the center of beads.

When working bullion stitch, after drawing yarn through indicated stitch, let the yarn relax for a second before completing the stitch.

Maintain a fairly loose tension. Relax your tension hand a little before drawing through the loops.

When drawing the yarn through the loops, try holding the hook open side down the first 2 stitches, and then rotate the hook so the open side is facing up to draw through the remaining loops.

SPECIAL STITCHES

Bullion stitch (bullion st): Wrap yarn around hook indicated number of times, insert hook in indicated st, yo, draw up a lp, yo and gently draw through all lps on hook, yo, do not draw up tight, ch 1 to lock st.

Romanian point lace cord: Sc in 2nd ch from hook, rotate piece away from you *(always rotate in the same direction)*, sc in single lp of last ch made, rotate choker away from you until you are looking at the back side of choker, you will now see 2 lps at base of the last sc made, these will be to the side and toward the top, 1 sc worked in these 2 lps, *rotate choker away from you, sc in 2 lps at base of previous sc, rep from * until desired length of cord.

Picot: Ch 3, sl st in top of last dc made.

Double treble cluster (dtr cl): [Yo hook 3 times, insert hook in indicated ch, yo, draw up a lp, (yo, draw through 2 lps on hook) 3 times] 3 times, yo, draw through all 4 lps on hook.

NECKLACE
FLOWER

Rnd 1: With size 7 hook and antique violet medium, ch 4, **join** (see Pattern Notes) in first ch, ch 1, 15 sc in ring, join in beg sc. (15 sc)

Rnd 2: Ch 1, working in **front lp** (see Stitch Guide), sc in same st as beg ch-1, ch 2, [sc in next sc, ch 2] around, join in beg sc. Fasten off. (15 sc, 15 ch-2 sps)

Rnd 3: Working in **back lp** (see Stitch Guide) of each st around, join ocean teal medium in back lp of any rem back lp of rnd 1, ch 1, sc in same st, sc in each rem st around, join in front lp of beg sc. (15 sc)

Rnd 4: (Ch 4, 12-wrap **bullion st**—see Special Stitches) in same sc, (working in front lp, 15-wrap bullion st, ch 2, sl st into top of bullion st) in next sc, (12-wrap bullion st, ch 4, sl st) in next sc, [sl st in next sc, (ch 4, 12-wrap bullion st) in next sc, (15-wrap bullion st, ch 2, sl st into top of bullion st) in next sc, (12-wrap bullion st, ch 4, sl st) in next sc] around. Fasten off.

DANGLES

With size 7 hook, join antique violet medium in rem back lp of last st on any petal of rnd 3 of Flower, ch 10, (4 dc, **picot**—see Special Stitches, 2 dc, ch 1, sl st) in 2nd ch from hook, sl st in each of next 8 chs, sl st in back lp of the same st on rnd 3 of Flower, sl st in first back lp of next petal, ch 12, (4 dc, picot, 2 dc, ch 1, sl st) in 2nd ch from hook, sl st in each of next 10 chs, sl st in back lp of same sc on rnd 3 of Flower. Fasten off.

FIRST LEAF

With size 7 hook, join leaf green dark in back lp of sc before first Dangle in rem back lp on rnd 3 of Flower, ch 5, holding the last lp of each st on the hook, **dtr cl** (see Special Stitches) in 4th ch from hook, ch 5, sl st in same 4th ch as cl was worked, sl st in next ch, sl st in back lp of same sc on Flower. Fasten off.

2ND LEAF

With size 7 hook, join leaf green dark in back lp of sc after 2nd Dangle in rem back lp on rnd 3 of Flower, ch 5, holding the last lp of each st on the hook, dtr cl in 4th ch from hook, ch 5, sl st in same 4th ch as cl was worked, sl st in next ch, sl st in back lp of same sc on Flower. Fasten off.

CHOKER

With size 7 hook and antique violet medium, ch 2, (4 dc, picot in last dc made, 2 dc, ch 1, sl st) in 2nd ch from hook, make a ch 16 [28, 20] inches long, change to size 5 hook, work **Romanian point lace cord** (see Special Stitches), rep until desired length of Choker, ch 2, (4 dc, picot in last dc made, 2 dc, ch 1, sl st) in 2nd ch from hook. Fasten off.

FINISHING

Mark center of Choker, making sure cord doesn't twist, cross the Choker about 2 inches on each side up from center, sew the Choker tog where it crosses. Sew Flower to Choker where it crosses.

Sew 4 mm bead to center of Flower.

Sew 2mm bead at the base of dc sts on each of the 2 Dangles below Flower and on each end of the Choker. ∎

Renaissance
Shawlette

SKILL LEVEL

EXPERIENCED

FINISHED SIZE
17 inches long x 46 inches wide

MATERIALS
- Premier Yarns Deborah Norville Serenity Sock fine (sport) weight rayon/merino/nylon yarn (1¾ oz/230 yds/107g per ball):
    3 balls #2502 violas
- Size G/6/4mm in-line crochet hook or size needed to obtain gauge
- Tapestry needle
- 24mm button

GAUGE
[Bullion st, ch 1] 8 times = 3 inches; 5 bullion rows =2¾ inches

PATTERN NOTES
Weave in loose ends as work progresses.

When working bullion stitch, after drawing yarn through indicated stitch, let the yarn relax for a second before completing the stitch.

Maintain a fairly loose tension. Relax your tension hand a little before drawing through the loops.

When drawing the yarn through the loops, try holding the hook open side down the first 2 stitches, and then rotate the hook so the open side is facing up to draw through the remaining loops.

Chain-2 at beginning of row counts as first double crochet unless otherwise stated.

Chain-3 at beginning of row counts as first double crochet and chain 1 unless otherwise stated.

Chain-5 at beginning of row counts as first double treble crochet unless otherwise stated.

SPECIAL STITCHES
Lover's knot (lk): Draw up a lp of indicated length, yo, draw through lp just made, sc between the lp and the single strand of thread or yarn. This will lock your stitch. Try to be consistent in the length of yarn that is drawn up. Make another lk and sc in indicated st to form the first inverted V. On the next row or rnd, work a bullion st and sc into the sc at the top of the inverted V. Make 2 more lk and sc in the sc at the top of the next inverted V. This will be repeated a required number of times.

Bullion stitch (bullion st): Wrap yarn around hook indicated number of times, insert hook in indicated st, yo, draw up a lp, yo and gently draw through all lps on hook, yo, do not draw up tight, ch 1 to lock the st.

Picot: Ch 3, sl st in last st made.

Triple picot (tr picot): Ch 4, sl st in front lp at top of last st made and the front strand of the actual st of the same st, ch 5, sl st in the same st again, catching the front lp of first ch-4 lp where sl st in top of the st, ch 4, sl st in the same st again, catching the front lp of the first ch-4 lp and ch-5 lp where sl st in top of st was worked.

SHAWLETTE
YOKE

Row 1 (RS): Beg at neckline, ch 104, sc in 2nd ch from hook, sc in each of next 4 chs, hdc in each of next 5 chs, dc in each of next 83 chs, hdc in each of next 5 chs, sc in each of next 5 chs, turn. *(10 sc, 10 hdc, 83 dc)*

Row 2: Ch 1, sc in same st, [ch 2, sk next st, sc in next st] across, turn. *(51 ch-2 sps)*

Row 3: Ch 1, sc in first ch-2 sp, draw lp up about ¾ inch *(maintaining lp length throughout)*, complete **lk** *(see Special Stitches)*, work another lk, sk next ch-2 sp, [sc in next ch-2 sp, work 2 lk, sk next ch-2 sp] across, turn. *(25 double lk sts)*

Row 4: Ch 5 *(see Pattern Notes)*, work a lk, sc in next sc, [work 2 lk, sk next sc, sc in next sc] across, ending with a lk, **dtr** *(see Stitch Guide)* in sc at the beg of previous row, turn. *(24 double lk, 2 single lk)*

Row 5: Ch 1, sc in same st, [ch 4, sk next st, sc in next st] across, turn. *(25 ch-4 sps)*

Row 6: Ch 1, sc in same sc, [5 sc in next ch-4 sp, sc in next sc] across, turn. *(151 sc)*

Row 7: Ch 1, sc in same st, sc in each of next 6 sts, hdc in each of next 7 sts, dc in each of next 123 sts, hdc in each of next 7 sc, sc in each of next 7 sc, turn. *(14 sc, 14 hdc, 123 dc)*

Row 8: Ch 3 *(see Pattern Notes)*, sk next st, [8-wrap **bullion st** *(see Special Stitches)* in next st, ch 1] across, ending with dc in last sc of row, turn. *(74 bullion sts, 75 ch-1 sps)*

Row 9: Ch 1, sc in same st, 2 sc in each ch-1 sp across, turn. *(151 sc)*

Row 10: Ch 1, sc in same st, [ch 2, sk next sc, sc in next sc] across, turn. *(75 ch-2 sps)*

Row 11: Ch 1, sc in first ch-2 sp, make 2 lk, sk next ch-2 sp, [sc in next ch-2 sp, make 2 lk, sk next ch-2 sp] across, turn. *(37 double lk)*

Row 12: Ch 5, make a lk, sc in next sc, [make 2 lk sts, sk next sc, sc in next sc] across, ending with a lk st and dtr in sc at the beg of previous row, turn. *(36 double lk sts, 2 single lk sts)*

Row 13: Ch 1, sc in same sc, [ch 4, sk next sc, sc in next sc] across, turn. *(37 ch-4 sps)*

Row 14: Ch 1, sc in same sc, [5 sc in next ch-4 sp, sc in next sc] across, turn. *(223 sc)*

Row 15: Ch 2 *(see Pattern Notes)*, dc in each sc across, turn. *(223 dc)*

Row 16: Ch 3, [sk next dc, dc in next dc, ch 1] twice, [sk next dc, 8-wrap bullion st in next dc, ch 1] 7 times,

A. [sk next dc, dc in next dc, ch 1] 8 times, [sk next dc, 8-wrap bullion st in next dc, ch 1] 8 times;

B. [sk next dc, dc in next dc, ch 1] 8 times, [sk next dc, 8-wrap bullion st in next dc, ch 1] 9 times;

C. [sk next dc, dc in next dc, ch 1] 8 times, [sk next dc, 8-wrap bullion st in next dc, ch 1] 10 times;

D. [sk next dc, dc in next dc, ch 1] 8 times, [sk next dc, 8-wrap bullion st in next dc, ch 1] 9 times;

E. [sk next dc, dc in next dc, ch 1] 8 times, [sk next dc, 8-wrap bullion st in next dc, ch 1] 8 times;

F. [sk next dc, dc in next dc, ch 1] 8 times, [sk next dc, 8-wrap bullion st in next dc, ch 1] 7 times;

G. [sk next dc, dc in next dc, ch 1] twice, sk next dc, dc in next dc, turn. *(58 bullion sts, 54 dc, 111 ch 1 sps)*

POINT NO. 1

Row 1: Sl st in first ch-1 sp, ch 3, [dc in next ch-1 sp, ch 1] twice, [8-wrap bullion st in next ch-1 sp, ch 1] 6 times, dc in next ch-1 sp, [ch 1, dc in next ch-1 sp] twice, turn. *(6 bullion sts, 6 dc, 11 ch-1 sps)*

Row 2: Sl st in first ch-1 sp, ch 3, [dc in next ch-1 sp, ch 1] twice, [8-wrap bullion st in next ch-1 sp, ch 1] 5 times, dc in next ch-1 sp, [ch 1, dc in next ch-1 sp] twice, turn. *(5 bullion sts, 6 dc, 10 ch-1 sps)*

Row 3: Sl st in first ch-1 sp, ch 3, [dc in next ch-1 sp, ch 1] twice, [8-wrap bullion st in next ch-1 sp, ch 1] 4 times, dc in next ch-1 sp, [ch 1, dc in next ch-1 sp] twice, turn. *(4 bullion sts, 6 dc, 9 ch-1 sps)*

Row 4: Sl st in first ch-1 sp, ch 3, [dc in next ch-1 sp, ch 1] twice, [8-wrap bullion st in next ch-1 sp, ch 1] 3 times, dc in next ch-1 sp, [ch 1, dc in next ch-1 sp] twice, turn. *(3 bullion sts, 6 dc, 8 ch-1 sps)*

Row 5: Sl st in first ch-1 sp, ch 3, [dc in next ch-1 sp, ch 1] twice, [8-wrap bullion st in next ch-1 sp, ch 1] twice, dc in next ch-1 sp, [ch 1, dc in next ch-1 sp] twice, turn. *(2 bullion sts, 6 dc, 7 ch-1 sps)*

Row 6: Sl st in first ch-1 sp, ch 3, [dc in next ch-1 sp, ch 1] twice, 8-wrap bullion st in next ch-1 sp, ch 1, dc in next ch-1 sp, [ch 1, dc in next ch-1 sp] twice, turn. *(1 bullion st, 6 dc, 6 ch-1 sps)*

Row 7: Sl st in first ch-1 sp, ch 3, [dc in next ch-1 sp, ch 1] 4 times, dc in next ch-1 sp, turn. *(6 dc, 5 ch-1 sps)*

Row 8: Sl st in first ch-1 sp, ch 3, [dc in next ch-1 sp, ch 1] 3 times, dc in next ch-1 sp, turn. *(5 dc, 4 ch-1 sps)*

Row 9: Sl st in first ch-1 sp, ch 3, [dc in next ch-1 sp, ch 1] twice, dc in next ch-1 sp, turn. *(4 dc, 3 ch-1 sps)*

Row 10: Sl st in first ch-1 sp, ch 3, dc in next ch-1 sp, ch 1, dc in next ch-1 sp, turn. *(3 dc, 2 ch-1 sps)*

Row 11: Sl st in first ch-1 sp, ch 3, dc in next ch-1 sp. Fasten off. *(2 dc, 1 ch-1 sp)*

POINT NO. 2

Row 1: Sk next 3 ch-1 sps on row 16 of Yoke, join in next ch-1 sp, ch 3, [dc in next ch-1 sp, ch 1] twice, [8-wrap bullion st in next ch 1 sp, ch 1] 7 times, dc in next ch-1 sp, [ch 1, dc in next ch 1 sp] twice, turn. *(7 bullion sts, 6 dc, 12 ch-1 sps)*

Row 2: Sl st in first ch-1 sp, ch 3, [dc in next ch-1 sp, ch 1] twice, [8-wrap bullion st in next ch-1 sp, ch 1] 6 times, dc in next ch-1 sp, [ch 1, dc in next ch-1 sp] twice, turn. *(6 bullion sts, 6 dc, 11 ch-1 sps)*

Rows 3–12: Rep rows 2–11 of Point No. 1. *(2 dc, 1 ch-1 sp)*

POINT NO. 3

Row 1: Sk next 3 ch-1 sps on row 16 of Yoke, join in next ch-1 sp, ch 3, [dc in next ch-1 sp, ch 1] twice, [8-wrap bullion st in next ch-1 sp, ch 1] 8 times, dc in next ch-1 sp, [ch 1, dc in next ch-1 sp] twice, turn. *(8 bullion sts, 6 dc, 13 ch-1 sps)*

Row 2: Sl st in first ch-1 sp, ch 3, [dc in next ch-1 sp, ch 1] twice, [8-wrap bullion st in next ch-1 sp, ch 1] 7 times, dc in next ch-1 sp, [ch 1, dc in next ch-1 sp] twice, turn. (*7 bullion sts, 6 dc, 12 ch-1 sps*)

Row 3: Sl st in first ch-1 sp, ch 3, dc in next ch-1 sp, ch 1] twice, [8-wrap bullion st in next ch-1 sp, ch 1] 6 times, dc in next ch-1 sp, [ch 1, dc in next ch-1 sp] twice, turn. (*6 bullion sts, 6 dc, 11 ch-1 sps*)

Rows 4–13: Rep rows 2–11 of Point No. 1. (*2 dc, 1 ch-1 sp*)

POINT NO. 4
Row 1: Sk next 3 ch-1 sps on row 16 of Yoke, join in next ch-1 sp, ch 3, [dc in next ch-1 sp, ch 1] twice, [8-wrap bullion st in next ch-1 sp, ch 1] 9 times, dc in next ch-1 sp, [ch 1, dc in next ch-1 sp] twice, turn. (*9 bullion sts, 6 dc, 14 ch-1 sps*)

Row 2: Sl st in first ch-1 sp, ch 3, [dc in next ch-1 sp, ch 1] twice, [8-wrap bullion st in next ch-1 sp, ch 1] 8 times, dc in next ch-1 sp, [ch 1, dc in next ch-1 sp] twice, turn. (*8 bullion sts, 6 dc, 13 ch-1 sps*)

Row 3: Sl st in first ch-1 sp, ch 3, [dc in next ch-1 sp, ch 1] twice, [8-wrap bullion st in next ch-1 sp, ch 1] 7 times, dc in next ch-1 sp, [ch 1, dc in next ch-1 sp] twice, turn. (*7 bullion sts, 6 dc, 12 ch-1 sps*)

Row 4: Sl st in first ch-1 sp, ch 3, [dc in next ch-1 sp, ch 1] twice, [8-wrap bullion st in next ch-1 sp, ch 1] 6 times, dc in next ch-1 sp, [ch 1, dc in next ch-1 sp] twice, turn. (*6 bullion sts, 6 dc, 11 ch-1 sps*)

Rows 5–14: Rep rows 2–11 of Point No. 1. (*2 dc, 1 ch-1 sp*)

POINT NO. 5
Rows 1–13: Rep rows 1–13 of Point No. 3.

POINT NO. 6
Rows 1–12: Rep rows 1–12 of Point No. 2.

POINT NO. 7
Row 1: Sk next 3 ch-1 sps on row 16 of Yoke, join in next ch-1 sp, ch 3, [dc in next ch-1 sp, ch 1] twice, [8-wrap bullion st in next ch-1 sp, ch 1] 6 times, dc in next ch-1 sp, [ch 1, dc in next ch-1 sp] twice, turn. (*6 bullion sts, 6 dc, 11 ch-1 sps*)

Rows 2–11: Rep rows 2–11 of Point No. 1.

POINT BORDER
Row 1: Join in first dc of row 15, ch 1, sc in same dc, work 2 lk sts, sc over post of dc on outside edge of row 1 of first point, [2 lk sts, sk next row, sc over post of dc of next row] 4 times, make 2 lk sts, sc in ch-1 sp of row 11, 2 lk sts, sc in same sp, make 2 lk sts, sc over post of dc of row 9 of inside edge of point, [2 lk sts, sk next row, sc over post of dc of next row] 4 times, 2 lk sts, sk next ch-1 sp on row 16, sc in next ch-1 sp,

A. 2 lk sts, sc over post of dc of outside edge of 2nd row of Point No. 2, [2 lk sts, sk next row, sc over post of dc of next row] 4 times, 2 lk sts, sc in next ch-1 sp of row 12, 2 lk sts, sc in same sp, 2 lk sts, sc over post of dc of row 10 of inside edge of point, [2 lk sts, sk next row, sc over post of dc of next row] 4 times, 2 lk sts, sk next ch-1 sp on row 16, sc in next ch-1 sp;

B. 2 lk sts, sc over post of dc of the outside edge of first row of Point No. 3, [2 lk sts, sk next row, sc over post of dc of next row] 5 times, 2 lk sts, sc in next ch-1 sp of row 13, 2 lk sts, sc in same sp;

C. 2 lk sts, sc over post of dc of row 11 of inside edge of point, [2 lk sts, sk next row, sc over post of dc of next row] 5 times, 2 lk sts, sk next ch-1 sp on row 16, sc in next ch-1 sp;

D. 2 lk sts, sc over post of dc of the outside edge of 2nd row of Point No. 4, [2 lk sts, sk next row, sc over post of dc of next row] 5 times, 2 lk sts, sc in the ch-1 sp of row 14, 2 lk sts, sc in same sp, 2 lk sts, sc over post of dc of row 12 of inside edge of point, [2 lk sts, sk next row, sc over post of dc of next row] 5 times, 2 lk sts, sk next ch-1 sp on row 16, sc in next ch-1 sp;

E. 2 lk sts, sc over post of dc of outside edge of first row of Point No. 5, [2 lk sts, sk next row, sc over post of dc of next row] 5 times, 2 lk sts, sc in next ch-1 sp of row 13, 2 lk sts, sc in same sp, 2 lk sts, sc over post of dc of row 11 of inside edge of point, [2 lk sts, sk next row, sc over post of dc of next row] 5 times, 2 lk sts, sk next ch-1 sp on row 16, sc in next ch-1 sp;

F. 2 lk sts, sc over post of dc of outside edge of 2nd row of Point No. 6, [2 lk sts, sk next row, sc over post of dc of next row] 4 times, 2 lk sts, sc in the ch-1 sp of row 12, 2 lk sts, sc in same sp;

G. 2 lk sts, sc over post of dc of row 10 of inside edge of point, [2 lk sts, sk next row, sc over post of dc of next row] 4 times, 2 lk sts, sk next ch-1 sp on row 16, sc in next ch-1 sp;

H. 2 lk sts, sc over post of dc of outside edge of first row of Point No. 7, [2 lk sts, sk next row, sc over post of dc of next row] 4 times, 2 lk sts, sc in ch-1 sp of row 11, 2 lk sts, sc in same sp, 2 lk sts, sc over post of dc of row 9 of inside edge of point, [2 lk sts, sk next row, sc over post of dc of next row] 4 times, 2 lk sts, sc in last dc on row 15, turn. *(97 double lk sts)*

Row 2: 2 lk sts, sc in next sc, {[2 lk sts, sk next sc, sc in next sc] 6 times, 2 lk sts, sc in same sc, [2 lk sts, sk next sc, sc in next sc] 6 times, sc in next sc} twice, {[2 lk sts, sk next sc, sc in next sc] 7 times, 2 lk sts, sc in same sc, [2 lk sts, sk next sc, sc in next sc] 7 times, sc in next sc} 3 times, [2 lk sts, sk next sc, sc in next sc] 6 times, 2 lk sts, sc in same sc, [2 lk sts, sk next sc, sc in next sc] 6 times, sc in next sc, [2 lk sts, sk next sc, sc in next sc] 6 times, 2 lk sts, sc in same sc, [2 lk sts, sk next sc, sc in next sc] 6 times, 2 lk sts, sc in next sc, turn. *(99 double lk sts)*

EDGING

Rnd 1: Ch 4, sc in next sc, [ch 5, sk next sc, sc in next sc] 7 times, ch 5, sc in same sc, [ch 5, sk next sc, sc in next sc] 6 times, sc in next sc, [ch 5, sk next sc, sc in next sc] 6 times, ch 5, sc in same sc, [ch 5, sk next sc, sc in next sc] 6 times, sc in next sc, {[ch 5, sk next sc, sc in next sc] 7 times, ch 5, sc in same sc, [ch 5, sk next sc, sc in next sc] 7 times, sc in next sc} 3 times, [ch 5, sk next sc, sc in next sc] 6 times, ch 5, sc in same sc, [ch 5, sk next sc, sc in next sc] 6 times, sc in next sc, [ch 5, sk next sc, sc in next sc] 6 times, ch 5, sc in same sc, [ch 5, sk next sc, sc in next sc] 7 times,

A. ch 1, tr in first dc of row 15, dc in last sc of row 14, 4 dc over ch-5 sp at beg of row 12, dc in next sc at end of row 11, dc in sc at beg of row 10, dc in sc at end of row 9, 3 dc over ch-3 at beg of row 8, dc in sc at end of row 7, dc in sc at beg of row 6, dc in sc at end of row 5, 4 dc over ch-5 sp at beg of row 4, dc in sc at end of row 3, dc in sc at beg of row 2;

B. dc in sc at beg of row 1, 2 sc in same sc, working in opposite side of foundation ch, sc in each st across, 2 sc in sc at end of row 1, dc in sc at beg of row 2, dc in sc at end of row 3, 4 dc over post of dtr at end of row 4, dc in sc at beg of row 5, dc in sc at end of row 6, dc in sc at beg of row 7, 3 dc over post of dc at end of row 8, dc in sc at beg of row 9, dc in sc at end of row 10, dc in sc at beg of row 11, 4 dc over post of dtr at end of row 12, dc in sc at beg of row 13, dc in sc at end of row 14, ending with sl st to join in 4th ch of beg ch-5, **do not turn.** *(99 ch-5 sps, 42 dc, 103 sc)*

Rnd 2: Ch 1, sc in same st, sc in ch-1 sp, [(sc, hdc, dc, **picot** —*see Special Stitches* in last dc made, 2 dc, **triple picot**—*see Special Stitches* in last dc made, 2 dc, picot in last dc made, hdc, sc) in next ch-5 sp] 7 times, working in next ch-5 sp at tip of point, (sc, hdc, dc, picot in last dc made, dc, 2 tr, picot in last tr made, 2 tr, triple picot in last tr made, 2 tr, picot in last tr made, 2 dc, picot in last dc made, hdc, sc) in ch-5 sp at tip of point, [(sc, hdc, dc, picot in last dc made, 2 dc, triple picot in last dc made, 2 dc, picot in last dc made, hdc, sc) in next ch-5 sp] 6 times, sc between next 2 sc,

A. [(sc, hdc, dc, picot in last dc made, 2 dc, triple picot in last dc made, 2 dc, picot in last dc made, hdc, sc) in next ch-5 sp] 6 times, working in next ch-5 sp at tip of point, (sc, hdc, dc, picot in last dc made, dc, 2 tr, picot in last tr made, 2 tr, triple picot in last tr made, 2 tr, picot in last tr made, 2 dc, picot in last dc made, hdc, sc) in ch-5 sp at tip of point, [(sc, hdc, dc, picot in last dc made, 2 dc, triple picot in last dc made, 2 dc, picot in last dc made, hdc, sc) in next ch-5 sp] 6 times, sc between next 2 sc;

B. *[(sc, hdc, dc, picot in last dc made, 2 dc, triple picot in last dc made, 2 dc, picot in last dc made, hdc, sc) in next ch-5 sp] 7 times, working in next ch-5 sp at tip of point, (sc, hdc, dc, picot in last dc made, dc, 2 tr, picot in last tr made, 2 tr, triple picot in last tr made, 2 tr, picot in last tr made, 2 dc, picot in last dc made, hdc, sc) in same ch-5 sp at tip of point, (sc, hdc, dc, picot in last dc made, 2 dc, triple picot in last dc made, 2 dc, picot in last dc made, hdc, sc) in next ch-5 sp] 7 times, sc between next 2 sc*, rep from * to * twice;

C. [(sc, hdc, dc, picot in last dc made, 2 dc, triple picot in last dc made, 2 dc, picot in last dc made, hdc, sc) in next ch-5 sp] 6 times, working in next ch-5 sp at tip of point, (sc, hdc, dc, picot in last dc made, dc, 2 tr, picot in last tr made, 2 tr, triple picot in last tr made, 2 tr, picot in last tr made, 2 dc, picot in last dc made, hdc, sc) in next ch-5 sp at tip of point, [(sc, hdc, dc, picot in last dc made, 2 dc, triple picot in last dc made, 2 dc, picot in last dc made, hdc, sc) in next ch-5 sp] 6 times, sc between next 2 sc;

D. [(sc, hdc, dc, picot in last dc made, 2 dc, triple picot in last dc made, 2 dc, picot in last dc made, hdc, sc) in ch-5 sp] 6 times, working in next ch-5 sp at tip of point, (sc, hdc, dc, picot in last dc made, dc, 2 tr, picot in last tr made, 2 tr, triple picot in last tr made, 2 tr, picot in last tr made, 2 dc, picot in last dc made, hdc, sc) in same ch-5 sp at tip of point, [(sc, hdc, dc, picot in last dc made, 2 dc, triple picot in last dc made, 2 dc, picot in last dc made, hdc, sc) in next ch-5 sp] 7 times;

E. sc in next ch-1 sp, sc in next dc, [sk next dc, 5 dc in next dc, sk next dc, sc in next dc] 4 times, sc in each of next 6 dc, ch 4, turn, sk next 3 sc, sc in next sc, sl st into next sc, ch 1, turn, 7 sc ch-4 sp, sc in next st (buttonhole), sc in first sc on top edge of shawl, picot in last sc made, [sc in next 2 sc, picot in last sc] 51 times, sc in next sc, sk next sc, 5 dc in next dc, sk next sc, [sc in next dc, sk next dc, 5 dc in next dc, sk next dc] 5 times, ending with sl st to join in first sc of rnd. Fasten off. *(94 picot edge points, 7 picot tip points, 9 groups of 5-dc, buttonhole, 52 picots on neckline edge)*

FINISHING
Sew button opposite buttonhole at neckline edge. Block Shawl. ∎

Winsome
Baby Blanket

SKILL LEVEL

INTERMEDIATE

FINISHED SIZE
37 inches square

MATERIALS
- Bernat Softee Baby light (light) worsted weight acrylic yarn (5 oz/ 362 yds/140g per ball):
  3 balls #02000 white
  2 balls #02004 mint
- Size F/5/3.75mm in-line crochet hook or size needed to obtain gauge
- Sewing needle
- White sewing thread
- 12mm white buttons: 4
- 4 x 10 x 10-inch square box
- Gold wrapping paper

GAUGE
Motif = 4 inches square

PATTERN NOTES
Weave in loose ends as work progresses.

Join with slip stitch as indicated unless otherwise stated.

When working bullion stitch, after drawing yarn through indicated stitch, let the yarn relax for a second before completing the stitch.

Maintain a fairly loose tension. Relax your tension hand a little before drawing through the loops.

When drawing the yarn through the loops, try holding the hook open side down the first 2 stitches, and then rotate the hook so the open side is facing up to draw through the remaining loops.

Chain-2 at beginning of round counts as first double crochet unless otherwise stated.

Chain-6 at beginning of round counts as first treble crochet and chain 2 unless otherwise stated.

SPECIAL STITCHES
Bullion stitch (bullion st): Wrap yarn around hook 7 times, insert hook in indicated st, yo, draw up lp, yo and gently draw through all lps on hook, yo, do not draw up tight, ch 1 to lock st.

Freestanding bullion stitch (freestanding bullion st): Make **slip ring** *(see illustration)*, wrap thread around hook 7 times, insert hook in indicated st, draw lp through, yo, draw through all lps on hook, do not draw up tight, ch 1 to lock st.

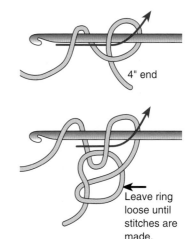

4" end

Leave ring loose until stitches are made.

Slip Ring

Front post bullion stitch (fp bullion st): Wrap yarn around hook 7 times, inserting hook front to back to front again around the vertical post of st on previous rnd, complete as a bullion st.

MOTIF PATTERN
MOTIF A
Rnd 1 (RS): With mint, ch 5, **join** (see Pattern Notes) in first ch, **ch 2** (see Pattern Notes), 11 dc in ring, join in 2nd ch of ch-2 at beg of rnd. (12 dc)

Rnd 2: Ch 2, **fp bullion st** (see Special Stitches) in each of next 2 dc, dc in next dc, ch 3, *dc in same dc, fp bullion st in each of next 2 dc**, dc in next dc, ch 3, rep from * around, ending last rep at **, dc in same dc as beg ch-2, ch 3, join in 2nd ch of beg ch-2. (8 fp bullion sts, 8 dc, 3 ch-3 sps)

Rnd 3: Ch 4, sk next 2 fp bullion sts, dc in next dc, (2 **bullion sts** (see Special Stitches), dc, ch 3, dc, 2 bullion sts) in next ch-3 sp, *dc in next dc, ch 2**, sk next 2 fp bullion sts, dc in next dc, (2 bullion sts, dc, ch 3, dc, 2 bullion sts) in next ch-3 sp, rep from * around, ending last rep at **, join in 2nd ch of beg ch-4. Fasten off. (16 bullion sts, 4 ch-2 sps, 4 ch-3 sps, 16 dc)

Rnd 4: Join white in first st of previous rnd, ch 2, *2 bullion sts in next ch-2 sp, dc in next dc, ch 2, sk next 2 bullion sts, dc in next dc, (2 bullion sts, dc, ch 3, dc, 2 bullion sts) in next ch-3 sp, dc in next dc, ch 2**, sk next 2 bullion sts, dc in next dc, rep from * around, ending last rep at **, join in beg ch-2. Fasten off. (24 bullion sts, 4 ch-3 sps, 8 ch-2 sps, 24 dc)

MOTIF B
ONE-SIDED JOINING
Rnds 1–3: Rep rnds 1–3 of Motif A.

Rnd 4: Join white in first st of previous rnd, ch 2, *2 bullion sts in next ch-2 sp, dc in next dc, ch 2, sk next 2 bullion sts, dc in next dc**, (2 bullion sts, dc, ch 3, dc, 2 bullion sts) in next ch-3 sp, dc in next dc, ch 2, sk next 2 bullion sts, dc in next dc, rep from * twice, ending 2nd rep at**, (2 bullion sts, dc, ch 1, sl st in adjacent ch-3 sp of Motif, ch 1, dc, 2 bullion sts) in ch-3 sp, dc in next dc, ch 1, sl st in adjacent ch-1 sp, ch 1, dc in next dc, 2 bullion sts in next ch-2 sp, dc in next dc, ch 1, sl st in adjacent ch-1 sp, dc in next dc, (2 bullion sts, dc, ch 1, sl st in adjacent ch-3 sp of Motif, ch 1, dc, 2 bullion sts) in ch-3 sp, dc in next dc, ch 2, join in beg ch-2. Fasten off. (24 bullion sts, 4 ch-3 sps, 8 ch-2 sps, 24 dc)

MOTIF C
2-SIDED JOINING
Rnds 1–3: Rep rnds 1–3 of Motif A.

Rnd 4: Join white in first st of previous rnd, ch 2, 2 bullion sts in next ch-2 sp, dc in next dc, ch 2, sk next 2 bullion sts, dc in next dc, (2 bullion sts, dc, ch 3, dc, 2 bullion sts) in next ch-3 sp, dc in next dc, ch 2, sk next 2 bullion sts, dc in next dc, 2 bullions in next ch-2 sp, dc in next dc, ch 2, sk next 2 bullions, dc in next dc, *(2 bullion sts, dc, ch 1, sl st in adjacent ch-3 sp of Motif, ch 1, dc, 2 bullion sts) in ch-3 sp, dc in next dc, ch 1, sl st in adjacent ch-1 sp, ch 1, dc in next dc, 2 bullion sts in next ch-2 sp, dc in next dc, ch 1, sl st in adjacent ch-1 sp, dc in next dc*, rep from * to * once, (2 bullion sts, dc, ch 1, sl st in adjacent ch-3 sp of Motif, ch 1, dc, 2 bullion sts) in ch-3 sp, dc in next dc, ch 2, join in beg ch-2. Fasten off. (24 bullion sts, 4 ch-3 sps, 8 ch-2 sps, 24 dc)

BABY BLANKET
MOTIFS 1–49
Working pattern of Motifs A, B and C, make 7 rows of 7 Motifs. Use care when joining that all bullions are on RS of Motifs as joined.

BORDER
Rnd 1 (RS): Join white in dc before first ch-2 sp after any corner and working toward next corner, ch 2, [2 bullion sts in ch-2 sp, dc in next dc, ch 2, dc in next dc] twice, bullion st in ch-3 sp on corner of motif, bullion st in next ch-3 sp of corner of next motif, dc in next dc, ch 2, dc in next dc, {[2 bullion sts in ch-2 sp, dc in next dc, ch 2, dc next dc] twice, bullion st in ch-3 sp on corner of motif, bullion st in next ch-3 sp of corner of next motif, dc in next dc, ch 2, dc in next dc} 5 times, [2 bullion sts in next ch-2 sp, dc in next dc, ch 2, dc in next dc] twice, (2 bullion sts, dc, ch 3, dc, 2 bullion sts) in next ch-3 sp, dc in next dc, ch 2, dc in next dc *{[2 bullion sts in ch-2 sp, dc in next dc, ch 2, dc next dc] twice, bullion st in ch-3 sp on corner of motif, bullion st in next ch-3 sp of corner of next motif, dc in next dc, ch 2, dc in next dc} 6 times, [2 bullion sts in next ch-2 sp, dc in next dc, ch 2, dc in next dc] twice, (2 bullion sts, dc, ch 3, dc, 2 bullion sts) in next ch-3 sp, dc in next dc, ch 2**, dc in next dc, rep from * around, ending last rep at **, join in beg ch-2. Fasten off.

Rnd 2: Join mint in dc before first ch-2 sp after any corner and working toward next corner, ch 2, *[2 bullion sts in ch-2 sp, dc in next dc, ch 2, dc next dc] 21 times, (2 bullion sts, dc, ch 3, dc, 2 bullion sts) in corner ch-3 sp, dc in next dc, ch 2**, dc in next dc, rep from * around, ending last rep at **, join in beg ch-2.

Rnd 3: Ch 4, *dc in next dc, [2 bullion sts in next ch-2 sp, dc in next dc, ch 2, dc next dc] 21 times, (2 bullion sts, dc, ch 3, dc, 2 bullion sts) in next corner ch-3 sp, dc in next dc, ch 2, 2 bullion sts in next ch-2 sp**, dc in next dc, ch 2, rep from * around, ending last rep at **, join in 2nd ch of beg ch-4. Fasten off.

Rnd 4: Join white in dc before corner ch-3 sp, ch 2, *(2 bullion sts, dc, ch 3, dc, 2 bullion sts) in corner ch-3 sp, dc in next dc, ch 2, dc in next dc, [2 bullion sts in next ch-2 sp, dc in next dc, ch 2**, dc in next dc] across to next corner ch-3 sp, rep from * around, ending last rep at **, join in beg ch-2.

Rnd 5: Ch 2, *(2 bullion sts, dc, ch 3, dc, 2 bullion sts) in corner ch-3 sp, dc in next dc, ch 2, dc in next dc, [2 bullion sts in next ch-2 sp, dc in next dc, ch 2**, dc in next dc] across to next corner ch-3 sp, rep from * around, ending last rep at **, join in beg ch-2.

Rnd 6: Sl st in corner ch-3 sp, **ch 6** *(see Pattern Notes)*, (tr, ch 3, tr, ch 2, tr) in same corner ch-3 sp, *ch 2, sc between next 2 bullion sts, ch 2, [(tr, ch 3, tr) in next ch-2 sp, ch 2, sc between next 2 bullion sts, ch 2] rep across to next corner ch-3 sp**, (tr, ch 2, tr, ch 3, tr, ch 2, tr) in corner ch-3 sp, rep from * around, ending last rep at **, join in 4th ch of beg ch-6. Fasten off.

Rnd 7: With white, work **freestanding bullion st** *(see Special Stitches)* in first ch-3 sp on any side edge, 3 bullion sts in same ch-3 sp, *work 4 bullion sts in each ch-3 sp across edge to first corner ch-2 sp, 2 bullion sts in next corner ch-2 sp, 5 bullion sts in next corner ch-3 sp, 2 bullion sts in next corner ch-2 sp, rep from * around, join in beg freestanding bullion st. Fasten off.

Rnd 8: Attach mint in any sp between bullion sts, ch 1, [sc in next sp between bullion sts, ch 3] rep around outer edge, join in beg sc. Fasten off.

With WS facing, block Blanket. ■

Snow Birds
Scarf, Hat & Mitts

SKILL LEVEL

INTERMEDIATE

FINISHED SIZES
Scarf: 4 inches wide x 64 inches long

Hat: 26½ inches in circumference

Mitts: 4 inches wide x 6 inches long

MATERIALS
- Patons Beehive Baby Sport light (light) worsted weight acrylic yarn (3½ oz/359 yds/100g per ball): 3 balls #09007 vintage lace
- Size F/5/3.75mm in-line crochet hook or size needed to obtain gauge
- Tapestry needle

GAUGE
8 rnds = 2½ inches; 16 sts = 2½ inches

PATTERN NOTES
Weave in loose ends as work progresses.

Join with slip stitch as indicated unless otherwise stated.

When working bullion stitch, after drawing yarn through indicated stitch, let the yarn relax for a second before completing the stitch.

Maintain a fairly loose tension. Relax your tension hand a little before drawing through the loops.

When drawing the yarn through the loops, try holding the hook open side down the first 2 stitches, and then rotate the hook so the open side is facing up to draw through the remaining loops.

Chain-2 at beginning of round counts as first double crochet unless otherwise stated.

Chain-4 at beginning of round counts as first double crochet and chain 2 unless otherwise stated.

Chain-5 at beginning of round counts as first double crochet and chain 3 unless otherwise stated.

Chain-7 at beginning of round counts as first double crochet and chain 5 unless otherwise stated.

Chain-8 at beginning of round counts as first double crochet and chain 6 unless otherwise stated.

SPECIAL STITCHES
Bullion stitch (bullion st): Wrap yarn around hook indicated number of times, insert hook in indicated st, yo, draw up a lp, yo and gently draw through all lps on hook, yo, do not draw up tight, ch 1 to lock st.

Picot: Ch 3, sl st in top of last dc made.

SCARF
Rnd 1: Ch 48, **join** (see Pattern Notes) to form ring, using care not to twist ch, **ch 2** (see Pattern Notes), dc in each ch st around, join in beg ch-2. (48 dc)

Rnd 2: Ch 2, **bpdc** (see Stitch Guide) in next dc, [**fpdc** (see Stitch Guide) in next dc, bpdc in next dc] around, join in beg ch-2. (24 fpdc, 24 bpdc)

Rnds 3–5: Ch 2, bpdc in next bpdc, [fpdc in next fpdc, bpdc in next bpdc] around, join in beg ch-2.

Rnd 6: Ch 5 (see Pattern Notes), sk each of next bpdc and fpdc, sc in next bpdc, ch 3, sk each of next fpdc and bpdc, dc in next fpdc, dc in next bpdc, [dc in next fpdc, ch 3, sk each of next bpdc and fpdc, sc in next bpdc, ch 3, sk each of next fpdc and bpdc, dc in next fpdc, dc in next bpdc] around, join in 2nd ch of beg ch-5. (18 dc, 12 ch-3 sps, 6 sc)

Rnd 7: Ch 8 (see Pattern Notes), dc in next dc, 10-wrap **bullion st** (see Special Stitches) in next dc, [dc in next dc, ch 6, dc in next dc, 10-wrap bullion st in next dc] around, join in 2nd ch of beg ch-8. (12 dc, 6 bullion sts, 6 ch-6 sps)

Rnd 8: Ch 4 (see Pattern Notes), sc in next ch-6 sp, ch 2, dc in next dc, fpdc around next bullion st, [dc in next dc, ch 2, sc in next ch-6 sp, ch 2, dc in next dc, fpdc around next bullion st] around, join in 2nd ch of beg ch-4. (12 dc, 6 fpdc, 6 sc, 12 ch-2 sps)

Rnd 9: Ch 2, 2 dc in next ch-2 sp, 10-wrap bullion st worked over the sc of previous rnd and ch-6 of 2 rnds before, 2 dc in next ch-2 sp, dc in next dc, dc in next fpdc, [dc in next dc, 2 dc in next ch-2 sp, 10-wrap bullion st worked over sc of previous rnd and ch-6 of 2 rnds before, 2 dc in next ch-2 sp, dc in next dc, dc in next fpdc] around, join in 2nd ch of beg ch-2. (42 dc, 6 bullions sts)

Rnd 10: Ch 5, sk next 2 dc, **fpsc** (see Stitch Guide) around bullion st, ch 3, sk next 2 dc, dc in next 2 dc, [dc in next dc, ch 3, sk next 2 dc, fpsc around bullion st, ch 3, sk next 2 dc, dc in next 2 dc] around, join in 2nd ch of beg ch-5. (18 dc, 6 fpsc, 12 ch-3 sps)

Rnd 11: Rep rnd 7.

Rnd 12: Rep rnd 8.

Rnds 13–152: [Rep rnds 9–12 consecutively] 35 times.

Rnd 153: Ch 2, 2 dc in next ch-2 sp, dc over sc of previous rnd and ch-6 of 2 rnds before, 2 dc in next ch-2 sp, dc in next dc, dc in next fpdc, [dc in next dc, 2 dc in next ch-2 sp, dc over sc of previous rnd and ch-6 of 2 rnds before, 2 dc in next ch-2 sp, dc in next dc, dc in next fpdc] around, join in 2nd ch of beg ch-2. (48 dc)

Rnd 154: Ch 2, bpdc in next dc [fpdc in next dc, bpdc in next dc] around, join in beg ch-2.

Rnds 155–157: Ch 2, bpdc in next bpdc, [fpdc in next fpdc, bpdc in next bpdc] around, join in beg ch-2.

FIRST BORDER
Rnd 158: Ch 1, sc in same st, ch 5, sk each of next bpdc, fpdc and bpdc, [sc in next fpdc, ch 5, sk each of next bpdc, fpdc and bpdc] around, join in beg sc.

Rnd 159: Sl st into next ch-5 sp, ch 1, 2 sc in same sp, ch 8, (3 dc, **picot**—*see Special Stitches*, 2 dc, ch 2, sl st) in 2nd ch from hook, sl st in each of next 6 ch sts, 2 sc in same ch-5 sp, ch 10, (3 dc, picot, 2 dc, ch 2, sl st) in 2nd ch from hook, sl st in each of next 8 ch sts, 2 sc in same ch-5 sp, [2 sc in next ch-5 sp, ch 8, (3 dc, picot, 2 dc, ch 2, sl st) in 2nd ch from hook, sl st in each of next 6 ch sts, 2 sc in same ch-5 sp, sl st in each of next 6 chs, 2 sc in same ch-5 sp, ch 10, (3 dc, picot, 2 dc, ch 2, sl st) in 2nd ch from hook, sl st in each of next 8 ch sts, 2 sc in same ch-5 sp] rep around, join in beg sc. Fasten off.

2ND BORDER
Rnd 158: Join yarn in opposite side of foundation ch of rnd 1 in base of first fpdc, sk each of next bpdc, fpdc, and bpdc, [sc in foundation ch of base of next fpdc, ch 5, sk each of next bpdc, fpdc and bpdc] rep around, join in beg sc.

Rnd 159: Rep rnd 159 of First Border.

FLOWER
MAKE 2.
Rnd 1: Leaving 10-inch length at beg, ch 4, join to form a ring, ch 1, 12 sc in ring, join in beg sc. *(12 sc)*

Rnd 2: Ch 1, sc in same sc, ch 3, sk next sc, [sc in next sc, ch 3, sk next sc] around, join in beg sc. *(6 ch-3 sps)*

Rnd 3: Ch 1, [(sc, 5 dc, sc) in next ch-3 sp] 6 times, join in beg sc. Fasten off.

Position flower on ribbing on end of scarf where desired. Using 10-inch tail, sew in place.

LEAF
MAKE 4.
Ch 6, 2 sc in 2nd ch from hook, hdc in next ch, 3 dc in next ch, hdc in next ch, (2 sc, picot in last sc made, sc) in next ch, working in opposite side of foundation ch, hdc in next ch, 3 dc in next ch, hdc in next ch, sc in next ch, join in beg sc. Leaving 10-inch length, fasten off.

With rem length, sew 2 Leaves next to each Flower as desired.

HAT
Rnd 1: Beg at crown of Hat, ch 5, join in first ch to form a ring, ch 2, 15 dc in ring, join in beg ch-2. *(16 dc)*

Rnd 2: Ch 2, dc in same st, [fpdc in next dc, dc in same st] around, join in beg ch-2. *(16 fpdc, 16 dc)*

Rnd 3: Ch 2, 2 dc in next dc, [fpdc in next fpdc, 2 dc in next dc] around, join in beg ch-2. *(16 fpdc, 32 dc)*

Rnd 4: Ch 2, dc in next dc, fpdc in same dc, dc in next dc, [fpdc in next fpdc, dc in next dc, fpdc in same dc, dc in next dc] around, join in beg ch-2. *(32 fpdc, 32 dc)*

Rnd 5: Ch 2, dc in next dc, 2 fpdc in next fpdc, dc in next dc, [fpdc in next fpdc, dc in next dc, 2 fpdc in next fpdc, dc in next dc] around, join in beg ch-2. *(48 fpdc, 32 dc)*

Rnd 6: Ch 2, dc in next dc, fpdc in next fpdc, 10-wrap bullion st in sp between last fpdc and next fpdc, fpdc in next fpdc, dc in next dc, [fpdc in next fpdc, dc in next dc, fpdc in next fpdc, 10-wrap bullion st in sp between last fpdc and next fpdc, fpdc in next fpdc, dc in next dc] around, join in beg ch-2. *(48 fpdc, 32 dc, 16 bullion sts)*

Rnd 7: Ch 2, 2 dc in next dc, [fpdc in next fpdc] twice, 2 dc in next dc, *fpdc in next fpdc, 2 dc in next dc, [fpdc in next fpdc] twice, 2 dc in next dc, rep from * around, join in beg ch-2. *(48 fpdc, 64 dc)*

Rnd 8: Ch 2, dc in each of next 2 dc, 1 fpdc around next 2 fpdc, dc in each of next 2 dc, [fpdc in next fpdc, dc in each of next 2 dc, 1 fpdc around next 2 fpdc, dc in each of next 2 dc] around, join in beg ch-2. *(32 fpdc, 64 dc)*

Rnd 9: Ch 2, dc in each of next 2 dc, fpdc in next fpdc, fpdc in same fpdc, dc in each of next 2 dc, [fpdc in next fpdc, dc in each of next 2 dc, fpdc in next fpdc, fpdc in same fpdc, dc in each of next 2 dc] around, join in beg ch-2. *(48 fpdc, 64 dc)*

Rnd 10: Ch 2, dc in each of next 2 dc, fpdc in next fpdc, 10-wrap bullion st between last fpdc and next fpdc, fpdc in next fpdc, dc in each of next 2 dc, [fpdc in next fpdc, dc in each of next 2 dc, fpdc in next fpdc, 10-wrap bullion st between last fpdc and next fpdc, fpdc in next fpdc, dc in each of next 2 dc] around, join in beg ch-2. *(48 fpdc, 64 dc, 16 bullion sts)*

Rnd 11: Ch 2, dc in each of next 2 dc, fpdc in next fpdc, fpdc in next fpdc, dc in each of next 2 dc, [fpdc in next fpdc, dc in each of next 2 dc, fpdc in next fpdc, fpdc in next fpdc, dc in each of next 2 dc] around, join in beg ch-2. *(48 fpdc, 64 dc)*

Rnd 12: Ch 2, dc in each of next 2 dc, 1 fpdc around next 2 fpdc, dc in each of next 2 dc, [fpdc in next fpdc, dc in each of next 2 dc, 1 fpdc around next 2 fpdc, dc in each of next 2 dc] around, join in beg ch-2. *(32 fpdc, 64 dc)*

Rnd 13: Ch 5, fpsc in next fpdc, ch 3, sk next dc, dc in next dc, fpdc in next fpdc, [dc in next dc, ch 3, fpsc in next fpdc, ch 3, sk next dc, dc in next dc, fpdc in next fpdc] around, join in 2nd ch of beg ch-5. *(32 dc, 16 fpdc, 16 fpsc, 32 ch-3 sps)*

Rnd 14: Ch 7 *(see Pattern Notes)*, dc in next dc, 10-wrap bullion st in next fpdc, [dc in next dc, ch 5, dc in next dc, 10-wrap bullion st in next fpdc] around, join in 2nd ch of beg ch-7. *(32 dc, 16 bullion sts, 16 ch-5 sps)*

Rnd 15: Ch 4, sc in next ch-5 sp, ch 2, dc in next dc, fpdc around next bullion st, [dc in next dc, ch 2, sc in next ch-5 sp, ch 2, dc in next dc, fpdc around next bullion st] around, join in 2nd ch of beg ch-4. *(16 fpdc, 32 dc, 32 ch-2 sps, 16 sc)*

Rnd 16: Ch 2, dc in next ch-2 sp, 10-wrap bullion st worked over the sc of previous rnd and ch-5 of rnd 14, dc in next ch-2 sp, dc in next dc, dc in next fpdc, [dc in next dc, dc in next ch-2 sp, 10-wrap bullion st worked over sc of previous rnd and the ch-5 of rnd 14, dc in next ch-2 sp, dc in next dc, dc in next fpdc, join in beg ch-2. *(16 bullion sts, 16 fpdc, 64 dc)*

Rnd 17: Ch 5, sk next dc, fpsc around next bullion st, ch 3, sk next dc, dc in each of next 2 dc, [dc in next dc, ch 3, sk next dc, fpsc around bullion st, ch 3, sk next dc, dc in each of next 2 dc] around, join in 2nd ch of beg ch-5. *(48 dc, 32 ch-3 sps)*

Rnd 18: Ch 7, dc in next dc, 10-wrap bullion st in next dc, [dc in next dc, ch 5, dc in next dc, 10-wrap bullion st in next dc] around, join in 2nd ch of beg ch-7. *(32 dc, 16 bullion sts)*

Rnd 19: Ch 4, sc in next ch-5 sp, ch 2, dc in next dc, fpdc around next bullion st, [dc in next dc, ch 2, sc in next ch-5 sp, ch 2, dc in next dc, fpdc around next bullion st] around, join in 2nd ch of beg ch-4. *(32 dc, 16 fpdc)*

Rnd 20: Ch 2, (2 dc in next ch-2 sp) twice, dc in next dc, dc in next fpdc, [dc in next dc, (2 dc in next ch 2 sp) twice, dc in next dc, dc in next fpdc] around, join in 2nd ch of beg ch-2. *(112 dc)*

Rnd 21: Ch 2, bpdc in next dc, [fpdc in next dc, bpdc in next dc] around, join in 2nd ch of beg ch-2.

Rnds 22–24: Ch 2, bpdc in next bpdc, [fpdc in next fpdc, bpdc in next bpdc] around, join in beg ch-2. At the end of rnd 24, fasten off.

FLOWER & LEAF TRIM
Make 1 Flower and 2 Leaves for Hat the same as for Scarf. Position Flower centered on ribbing on bottom edge of Hat as desired. With rem length, sew Flower to Hat. With rem length, sew a Leaf to each side of Flower as desired.

DANGLES
With vintage lace, ch 8, (3 dc, picot, 2 dc, ch 2, sl st) in 2nd ch from hook, sl st in each of next 6 ch sts, ch 10, (3 dc, picot, 2 dc, ch 2, sl st) in 2nd ch from hook, sl st in each of next 8 ch sts. Leaving 5 inch length, fasten off. With rem length, sew to center bottom under Flower.

FINGERLESS MITTS
MAKE 2.
Rnd 1: Ch 32, join to form a ring, using care not to twist ch, ch 2, dc in each ch around, join in beg ch-2. *(32 dc)*

Rnd 2: Ch 2, bpdc in next dc, [fpdc in next dc, bpdc in next dc] around, join in beg ch-2.

Rnds 3 & 4: Ch 2, bpdc in next bpdc, [fpdc in next fpdc, bpdc in next bpdc] around, join in beg ch-2.

Rnd 5: Ch 2, fpdc in same st, bpdc in next bpdc, [fpdc next fpdc, fpdc in same fpdc, bpdc in next bpdc] around, join in beg ch-2. *(32 fpdc, 16 bpdc)*

Rnd 6: Ch 5, sk next fpdc, sk next bpdc, sc in next fpdc, ch 3, sk next fpdc, sk next bpdc, dc in each of next 2 fpdc, dc in next bpdc, ch 3, sk next 2 fpdc, sc in next bpdc,

A. ch 3, sk next 2 fpdc, dc in next bpdc, dc in each of next 2 fpdc, ch 3, sk next bpdc, sk next fpdc, sc in next fpdc, ch 3, sk next bpdc, sk next fpdc, dc in next fpdc, dc in bpdc, dc in next fpdc;

B. ch 3, sk next fpdc, sk next bpdc, sc in next fpdc, sk next fpdc, sk next bpdc, dc in each of next 2 fpdc, dc in next bpdc, ch 3, sk next 2 fpdc, sc in next bpdc, sk next 2 fpdc, dc in next bpdc, dc in each of next 2 fpdc;

C. ch 3, sk next bpdc, sk next fpdc, sc in next fpdc, sk next bpdc, sk next fpdc, dc in next fpdc, dc in next bpdc, join in 2nd ch of beg ch-5. *(18 dc, 6 sc, 12 ch-3 sps)*

Rnd 7: Ch 8, dc in next dc, 10-wrap bullion st in next dc, [dc in next dc, ch 6, dc in next dc, 10-wrap bullion st in next dc] around, join in 2nd ch of beg ch-8. *(12 dc, 6 bullion sts, 6 ch-6 sps)*

Rnd 8: Ch 4, sc in next ch-6 sp, ch 2, dc in next dc, fpdc around next bullion st, [dc in next dc, ch 2, sc in next ch-6 sp, ch 2, dc in next dc, fpdc around next bullion st] around, join in 2nd ch of beg ch-4. *(12 dc, 6 fpdc, 12 ch-2 sps)*

Rnd 9: Ch 2, 2 dc in next ch-2 sp, 10-wrap bullion st worked over sc of previous rnd and ch-6 of 2 rnds below, 2 dc in next ch-2 sp, dc in next dc, dc in next fpdc, [dc in next dc, 2 dc in next ch-2 sp, 10-wrap bullion st worked over sc of previous rnd and ch 6 of 2 rnds below, 2 dc in next ch-2 sp, dc in next dc, dc in next fpdc] around, join in beg ch-2. *(42 dc, 6 bullion sts)*

Rnd 10: Ch 5, sk next 2 dc, fpsc around bullion st, ch 3, sk next 2 dc, dc in each of next 2 dc, [dc in next dc, ch 3, sk next 2 dc, fpsc around bullion st, ch 3, sk next 2 dc, dc in each of next 2 dc] around, join in 2nd ch of beg ch-5. *(18 dc, 6 fpsc, 12 ch-3 sps)*

Rnd 11: Rep rnd 7.

Rnd 12: Rep rnd 8.

Rnd 13: Ch 2, dc in next ch-2 sp, 10-wrap bullion st worked over sc of previous rnd and ch 6 of rnd 11, dc in next ch-2 sp, dc in next dc, dc in next fpdc, [dc in next dc, dc in next ch-2 sp, 10-wrap bullion st worked over the sc of previous rnd and ch 6 of rnd 11, dc in next ch-2 sp, dc in next dc, dc in next fpdc] around, join in beg ch-2. *(30 dc, 6 bullion sts)*

Rnd 14: Ch 4, sk next dc, fpsc around bullion st, ch 2, sk next dc, dc in each of next 2 dc, [dc in next dc, ch 2, sk next dc, fpsc around bullion st, ch 2, sk next dc, dc in each of next 2 dc] around, join in 2nd ch of beg ch-5. *(18 dc, 6 fpsc, 12 ch-2 sps)*

Rnd 15: Ch 6, dc in next dc, 10-wrap bullion st in next dc, [dc in next dc, ch 4, dc in next dc, 10-wrap bullion st in next dc] around, join in 2nd ch of beg ch-6. *(12 dc, 6 bullion sts, 6 ch-4 sps)*

Rnd 16: Ch 3, sc in next ch-4 sp, ch 1, dc in next dc, fpdc around next bullion st, [dc in next dc, ch 1, sc in next ch-4 sp, ch 1, dc in next dc, fpdc around next bullion st] around, join in 2nd ch of beg ch-3. *(12 dc, 6 fpdc, 12 ch-1 sps, 6 sc)*

Rnd 17: Ch 2, [2 dc in next ch-1 sp] twice, dc in next dc, sk next fpdc, *dc in next dc, [2 dc in next ch-1 sp] twice, dc in next dc, sk next fpdc, rep from * around, join in 2nd ch of beg ch-2. *(36 dc)*

Rnd 18: Ch 2, bpdc in next dc, [fpdc in next dc, bpdc in next dc] around, join in 2nd ch of beg ch-2. *(36 sts)*

Rnd 19: Ch 2, bpdc in next bpdc, [fpdc in next fpdc, bpdc in next bpdc] 11 times, ch 1, sl st in 6th bpdc on same rnd, ch 1, sl st in top of last bpdc made *(opening for index finger formed)*, [fpdc in next fpdc, bpdc in next bpdc] 4 times, ch 1, sl st in the 3rd fpdc on same rnd, ch 1, sl st into top of last bpdc made *(opening for pinkie finger formed)*, [fpdc in next fpdc, bpdc in next bpdc] twice, join in 2nd ch of beg ch-2. Fasten off.

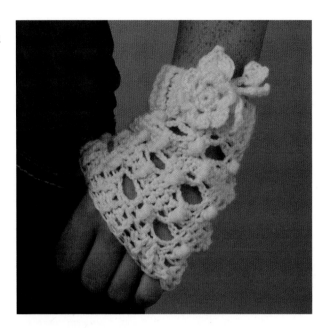

EMBELLISHMENT FOR MITTS
DANGLES MITT A
Join yarn in the 5th st on rnd 1, ch 6, (3 dc, picot, 2 dc, ch 2, sl st) in 2nd ch from hook, sl st in each of next 4 chs, sl st in same st on rnd 1, ch 8, (3 dc, picot, 2 dc, ch 2, sl st) in 2nd ch from hook, sl st in each of next 6 ch sts. Fasten off.

DANGLES MITT B
Join yarn in the 29th st on rnd 1, ch 6, (3 dc, picot, 2 dc, ch 2, sl st) in 2nd ch from hook, sl st in each of next 4 chs, sl st in same st on rnd 1, ch 8, (3 dc, picot, 2 dc, ch 2, sl st) in 2nd ch from hook, sl st in each of next 6 ch sts. Fasten off.

LEAF
MAKE 4.
Make Leaf same as for Scarf, sew 2 leaves next to dangles on 2nd rnd on thumb side of Dangle and on the 3rd rnd of little finger side of Dangle.

FLOWER
MAKE 2.
Make Flower same as for Scarf, position Flower over base end of Leaves and sew in place. ■

Metric Conversion Charts

METRIC CONVERSIONS

yards	x	.9144	=	metres (m)
yards	x	91.44	=	centimetres (cm)
inches	x	2.54	=	centimetres (cm)
inches	x	25.40	=	millimetres (mm)
inches	x	.0254	=	metres (m)

centimetres	x	.3937	=	inches
metres	x	1.0936	=	yards

INCHES INTO MILLIMETRES & CENTIMETRES (Rounded off slightly)

inches	mm	cm	inches	cm	inches	cm	inches	cm
1/8	3	0.3	5	12.5	21	53.5	38	96.5
1/4	6	0.6	5 1/2	14	22	56	39	99
3/8	10	1	6	15	23	58.5	40	101.5
1/2	13	1.3	7	18	24	61	41	104
5/8	15	1.5	8	20.5	25	63.5	42	106.5
3/4	20	2	9	23	26	66	43	109
7/8	22	2.2	10	25.5	27	68.5	44	112
1	25	2.5	11	28	28	71	45	114.5
1 1/4	32	3.2	12	30.5	29	73.5	46	117
1 1/2	38	3.8	13	33	30	76	47	119.5
1 3/4	45	4.5	14	35.5	31	79	48	122
2	50	5	15	38	32	81.5	49	124.5
2 1/2	65	6.5	16	40.5	33	84	50	127
3	75	7.5	17	43	34	86.5		
3 1/2	90	9	18	46	35	89		
4	100	10	19	48.5	36	91.5		
4 1/2	115	11.5	20	51	37	94		

KNITTING NEEDLES CONVERSION CHART

Canada/U.S.	0	1	2	3	4	5	6	7	8	9	10	10½	11	13	15
Metric (mm)	2	2¼	2¾	3¼	3½	3¾	4	4½	5	5½	6	6½	8	9	10

CROCHET HOOKS CONVERSION CHART

Canada/U.S.	1/B	2/C	3/D	4/E	5/F	6/G	8/H	9/I	10/J	10½/K	N
Metric (mm)	2.25	2.75	3.25	3.5	3.75	4.25	5	5.5	6	6.5	9.0

STITCH GUIDE

FOR MORE COMPLETE INFORMATION,
VISIT ANNIESCATALOG.COM/STITCHGUIDE

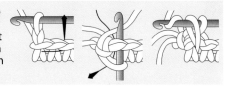

STITCH ABBREVIATIONS

beg	begin/begins/beginning
bpdc	back post double crochet
bpsc	back post single crochet
bptr	back post treble crochet
CC	contrasting color
ch(s)	chain(s)
ch-	refers to chain or space previously made (i.e., ch-1 space)
ch sp(s)	chain space(s)
cl(s)	cluster(s)
cm	centimeter(s)
dc	double crochet (singular/plural)
dc dec	double crochet 2 or more stitches together, as indicated
dec	decrease/decreases/decreasing
dtr	double treble crochet
ext	extended
fpdc	front post double crochet
fpsc	front post single crochet
fptr	front post treble crochet
g	gram(s)
hdc	half double crochet
hdc dec	half double crochet 2 or more stitches together, as indicated
inc	increase/increases/increasing
lp(s)	loop(s)
MC	main color
mm	millimeter(s)
oz	ounce(s)
pc	popcorn(s)
rem	remain/remains/remaining
rep(s)	repeat(s)
rnd(s)	round(s)
RS	right side
sc	single crochet (singular/plural)
sc dec	single crochet 2 or more stitches together, as indicated
sk	skip/skipped/skipping
sl st(s)	slip stitch(es)
sp(s)	space(s)/spaced
st(s)	stitch(es)
tog	together
tr	treble crochet
trtr	triple treble
WS	wrong side
yd(s)	yard(s)
yo	yarn over

YARN CONVERSION

OUNCES TO GRAMS		GRAMS TO OUNCES	
1	28.4	25	7/8
2	56.7	40	1⅓
3	85.0	50	1¾
4	113.4	100	3½

UNITED STATES		UNITED KINGDOM
sl st (slip stitch)	=	sc (single crochet)
sc (single crochet)	=	dc (double crochet)
hdc (half double crochet)	=	htr (half treble crochet)
dc (double crochet)	=	tr (treble crochet)
tr (treble crochet)	=	dtr (double treble crochet)
dtr (double treble crochet)	=	ttr (triple treble crochet)
skip	=	miss

Single crochet decrease (sc dec): (Insert hook, yo, draw lp through) in each of the sts indicated, yo, draw through all lps on hook.

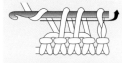

Example of 2-sc dec

Half double crochet decrease (hdc dec): (Yo, insert hook, yo, draw lp through) in each of the sts indicated, yo, draw through all lps on hook.

Example of 2-hdc dec

Reverse single crochet (reverse sc): Ch 1, sk first st, working from left to right, insert hook in next st from front to back, draw up lp on hook, yo, and draw through both lps on hook.

Chain (ch): Yo, pull through lp on hook.

Single crochet (sc): Insert hook in st, yo, pull through st, yo, pull through both lps on hook.

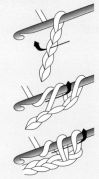

Double crochet (dc): Yo, insert hook in st, yo, pull through st, [yo, pull through 2 lps] twice.

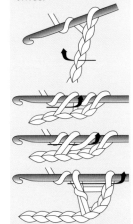

Double crochet decrease (dc dec): (Yo, insert hook, yo, draw lp through, yo, draw through 2 lps on hook) in each of the sts indicated, yo, draw through all lps on hook.

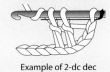

Example of 2-dc dec

Front loop (front lp) Back loop (back lp)

Front Loop   Back Loop

Front post stitch (fp): Back post stitch (bp): When working post st, insert hook from right to left around post of st on previous row.

Back   Front

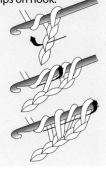

Post of Stitch

Half double crochet (hdc): Yo, insert hook in st, yo, pull through st, yo, pull through all 3 lps on hook.

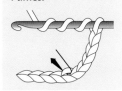

Double treble crochet (dtr): Yo 3 times, insert hook in st, yo, pull through st, [yo, pull through 2 lps] 4 times.

Treble crochet decrease (tr dec): Holding back last lp of each st, tr in each of the sts indicated, yo, pull through all lps on hook.

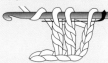

Example of 2-tr dec

Slip stitch (sl st): Insert hook in st, pull through both lps on hook.

Chain color change (ch color change) Yo with new color, draw through last lp on hook.

Double crochet color change (dc color change) Drop first color, yo with new color, draw through last 2 lps of st.

Treble crochet (tr): Yo twice, insert hook in st, yo, pull through st, [yo, pull through 2 lps] 3 times.

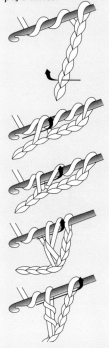

Annie's ™ *Beautiful Bullions* is published by Annie's, 306 East Parr Road, Berne, IN 46711. Printed in USA. Copyright © 2012 Annie's. All rights reserved. This publication may not be reproduced in part or in whole without written permission from the publisher.

RETAIL STORES: If you would like to carry this pattern book or any other Annie's publications, visit AnniesWSL.com

Every effort has been made to ensure that the instructions in this pattern book are complete and accurate. We cannot, however, take responsibility for human error, typographical mistakes or variations in individual work. Please visit AnniesCustomerCare.com to check for pattern updates.

ISBN: 978-1-59635-718-1

1 2 3 4 5 6 7 8 9